The Soul of Sponsorship

In gratitude to the anonymous donor from St. Paul, Minnesota, who supplied the funds for the production of this book.

The Soul of Sponsorship

THE FRIENDSHIP OF FATHER ED DOWLING, S.J. AND BILL WILSON IN LETTERS

by Robert Fitzgerald, S.J.

 Hazelden Publishing

Hazelden
Center City, Minnesota 55012-0176

21   18 19 20

Library of Congress Cataloging-in-Publication Data

Fitzgerald, Robert, 1935-
    The soul of sponsorship: the friendship of Father Ed Dowling and Bill Wilson in letters / Robert Fitzgerald.
    p. cm.
    Includes bibliographic references.
    ISBN 978-1-56838-084-1
    1. Dowling, Ed. 1898-1960. 2. W., Bill. 3. Spiritual biography-United States. 4. Alcoholics Anonymous—United States—Biography. 5. Alcoholics Anonymous. I. Dowling, Ed. 1898-1960. II. W., Bill. III. Title.
BL72.F55 1995
362.29'286'092273—dc20
[B]   95-9773
                                                              CIP

For Jo and Tom,

Jim and Ernie

A Ritual to Read to Each Other

If you don't know the kind of person I am
and I don't know the kind of person you are
a pattern that others made may prevail in the world
and following the wrong god home we may miss our star.

For there is many a small betrayal in the mind,
a shrug that lets the fragile sequence break
sending with shouts the horrible errors of childhood
storming out to play through the broken dyke.

And as elephants parade holding each elephant's tail,
but if one wanders the circus won't find the park,
I call it cruel and maybe the root of all cruelty
to know what occurs but not recognize the fact.

And so I appeal to a voice, to something shadowy,
a remote important region in all who talk:
though we could fool each other, we should consider—
lest the parade of our mutual life get lost in the dark.

For it is important that awake people be awake,
or a breaking line may discourage them back to sleep;
the signals we give—yes or no, or maybe—
should be clear: the darkness around us is deep.

—*William Stafford*
Stories That Could Be True
(New York: Harper & Row, 1977), p. 52.

Contents

Foreword

We live in a funny world. What used to be "Alcoholics Anonymous" became, first, "a Twelve-Step group" and then part of "the Recovery Movement." Many gained from those changes, but something was also lost...even in what remains Alcoholics Anonymous.

There have been other gains and losses. Within A.A., some have moved away from the practice of "sponsorship" — the great gift to the fellowship from its early Cleveland membership. In the wider world, as we emerge from the 1970s and 1980s — decades that observers have named "Me" and "Greed" respectively — there has been a perhaps greater loss: the ancient and indeed sacred understanding of *friend*. This is a 1990s book, a book about friendship.

The co-founders of Alcoholics Anonymous, William Griffith Wilson and Dr. Robert Holbrook Smith,[1] although both Vermont-born Yankees, were two very different individuals. Bill became a pushy New York promoter; Bob, a reserved midwestern surgeon. As many have observed, if they had met in a bar, they would probably not have chosen to drink together. But because they met while trying desperately to stay sober, and because they found that they could do that only "together," they gave the world a fellowship that has saved countless lives.

To a casual observer, Bill Wilson and Father Ed Dowling had even less in common. Although loosely Protestant in background, Bill had been raised without any religion. In prep school, in fact, in his despair over the death of his beloved Bertha Banford, Bill had decided that the universe made no sense. Too lazy to become a real atheist, he would later describe himself (and others) as "We Agnostics."

St. Louis-born and street-wise Eddie Dowling, meanwhile, not only came from an urban, immigrant Catholic background, he was a Catholic priest. And, worse than that to most Yankee-oriented Americans, he was a Jesuit — that mysterious Society of the Pope's loyal shock-troops, generally regarded by people of Bill's background as cunning, devious, and treacherous.

There were other differences. Wilson greatly admired and himself wanted to be one of the "number one" men, and those traits and that ambition endured into his sobriety. Dowling, as a seminarian, had humbly accepted being shunted off the Jesuit fast-track, judged intellectually deficient for his Society's crack positions on university faculties. Dowling, as a protegé of Father Daniel Lord, S.J., had a missionary's passion to spread his Catholic faith. Wilson emerged from his agnosticism to embrace "spirituality," not "religion." "The thing that irks me about all religion is how confoundedly right they all are," he wrote at the time he broke off his own investigation of Catholicism. Yet these two men learned more from each other than most of us gain from our most cherished teachers.

Bob Fitzgerald, in the pages that follow, uses the correspondence between the co-founder and the Jesuit to let us in on some of what they taught — and learned from — each other. For the letters Wilson and Dowling wrote each other lay bare the respect — the *love* — that bound together these two so different individuals. Their bond ran deep, and though Bill and Ed, like most American males, did not address the topic much directly, Fitzgerald deftly and respectfully explores their real bond: suffering. Using the metaphor of baseball, a game both men enjoyed, Bob Fitzgerald helps us understand the wider context of their understanding, which allowed them to bear up under suffering not only joyously but fruitfully.

"Pain is the touchstone of all growth," Bill Wilson reminded many members of Alcoholics Anonymous in his voluminous correspondence. Dowling spoke to his groups of Catholic married couples of "Glad Gethsemane," a paradoxical reference to the place of Christ's lonely agony just before his crucifixion. Neither idea attracts us in this era of bland uplift. But as a sidewalk scrawl by one of Bill's followers reminds: "Reality is for people who can't handle drugs." Wilson and Dowling had no need either to deny or to ignore suffering, their own or anyone else's.

Wisely, Fitzgerald attempts very little analysis; he does not even claim to tell us the full story of Wilson's and Dowling's rich relationship. Rather, following the example of his subjects, Bob accepts the limited task of making available to us, in context, their letters to each other. And perhaps because he follows so well the example of two men who lived traditions that he himself incorporates, from that acceptance of limitation there flow to us, his readers, richnesses that would have vanished under a heavier hand.

There are not only many "meditation books" today: there are too many. Squibs for "daily meditation" are useful, for beginners. But perhaps some are being locked into beginnerhood — into spiritual infancy: witness the vast concern bandied about over one's "inner child." The tradition tapped and lived by Bill Wilson and Ed Dowling makes available a spirituality, for maturing people. One way it has done that, for about two millennia, is through reading...but the reading of books, not pages. Meditation, like food, loses nutrients when it is canned.

This book, then, is the kind of meditation book we need: straightforward; respectful of both its subject and its readers; gently guiding only to remove obstacles, not to tell us what to think or, worse, how to feel. Wilson and Dowling and their friendship are well served by these pages. So, too, are we.

—Ernest Kurtz
January 6, 1994

Preface

"I do hope that a good biography comes out about Father Ed Dowling. He was made of the stuff of the saints," Bill W. wrote in a letter to a man who asked what Father Ed's sponsorship meant to Bill. "In a very real sense, he was my spiritual adviser, just as he was to many hundreds in AA."[2]

Five years earlier Bill had written to Anna, Father Ed Dowling's sister and secretary, "Have you ever thought of a book that someone might do, a biography of Father Ed? In my book he is a saint, and a most colorful one too. His benefactions to me are among my brightest memories."[3] This is not that biography.

I will focus on 195 letters between the two men. All but ten of the letters came from the Dowling archives of Maryville College in St. Louis; the other ten came from the New York AA Archives. These letters offer an intimate view of their twenty-year friendship.

I am drawn to tell this story. I feel close to both men. I trained as a Jesuit at St. Stanislaus Seminary in Florissant, Missouri, and at St. Louis University for arts and philosophy, the very same places Father Ed did his Jesuit training. I too, experienced the Ignatian vocation as mediated by the Missouri Province Jesuits. As I wrote this book, Father Ed's spirit mentored me.

I do feel close to Bill W., also. Since 1977 I have struggled with my own issues, many the same as Bill's.

I too have been helped by close friendships in recovery.

I will tell the story of their meeting, their backgrounds, and the twenty years of letters between them.

I want to celebrate their friendship.

Acknowledgments

Father Ed believed in baseball. James A. Egan, S.J., by his gift of his research on the letters, both invited me into the Dowling ballpark and stayed with me by phone and letter to the last inning. He introduced me to Mary Louise Adams, archivist emeritus of the Dowling collection at Maryville Library; Frank Mauser, archivist of the Bill W. collection at AAWS in New York; and Nell Wing, Bill W.'s secretary and AA's first archive director. All three loved and saved what these men wrote. Jim Egan also introduced me to Ernie Kurtz who kept with me chapter by chapter with his sensitivity for AA history and positive critiques. Without them, the book would have been called for darkness.

Others helped light the ballpark: Tom Book let me know what the friendship between two men can be, Jo Casey kept sending me on pilgrimage, the prunings of Matt Linn, S.J., gave the book life. Thanks to those from writing groups who stayed with me from first drafts: Joan Lovrien; Cindy Gustavson; Cathy Brown; and Linn Joslyn. They kept me swinging and taught me that errors are just part of coming home again. Barb Kast, John and Alice Jansen, and Joan Dillon helped me find a language to speak of discernment.

Thanks to Tom Leydon, who taught me the secret of leading off into first draft pronto. To Jane Howard at Split Rock Arts Program, who suggested the weakness of both men would be the "hole in the wall" where all could enter their ballpark. To Laurence Sutton, whose two Loft Classes gave me chapter deadlines and the suggestion of a book where the friendship lets each man be who he is. To John G. Scott, who hosted me in New York with stories about his cousin, Father Ed Dowling. To La Storta Jesuit community, my Minneapolis home, and to my homes away from home: the West Side Jesuit community in New York City and DeSmet community in St. Louis. Finally, I thank Bert Thelan, S.J., and the Wisconsin Province Jesuits, whose three-year grant allowed me the time to live with Father Ed Dowling as my mentor.

Going to bat with him at my elbow has been a precious three-year adventure. Somewhere this Irish catcher from Baden is taking a few hardballs from the boy who made the boomerang and pitched for Norwich Academy. I give thanks they met and played ball because — as in the film *Field of Dreams* — I can still hear their chatter and the call, "Batter up."

BILL WILSON   FATHER ED DOWLING

CHAPTER 1

Father Ed Meets Bill W.

That night, a cold damp November night in 1940, Bill W., co-founder of AA, had gone to bed. His feet were hanging over the end of the bed which nearly filled the small room he and his wife, Lois, had rented on the second floor of the 24th Street AA Club in New York City. Two orange crates with curtains served as their dresser. Hooks on the wall held their clothes. Lois supported them with her job at a department store. That night she was out somewhere. Cold rain and sleet were beating on the tin roof above him. Bill was wondering whether the pain he was feeling in his stomach was an ulcer.

The walls were closing in on him. Thousands of copies of the Big Book in Blackwell's warehouse were waiting, unsold. A few men were sober through AA. Bill was frustrated. How to reach all who wanted help? In February of that year the Rockefeller dinner with its gathering of some prominent New York friends of Rockefeller interested in AA had come and gone with applause and some small donations. Hank P., an early member, after complaining for half a year, finally got drunk in April. Rollie H., a nationally famous ballplayer, sobered up with the Cleveland group but broke anonymity by calling in the press for a full name and photograph story which became front-page news across the nation. Bill too began to give out pictures and interviews to reporters wherever he gave talks. Soon, he found his story and picture on Page One. Now *he* was becoming the center of attention. An old-timer in his New York group even accused him of being on a "dry drunk." Bill had just returned from Baltimore, where a minister had asked him to face the self-pity in his own talk. He was depressed. Bill wondered, "What was the use? What if I—five years sober—were to drink?"

It was ten P.M. that night when he heard the doorbell ringing through the empty club. Old Tom, the maintenance man, announced that there was "some bum from St. Louis" to see him.

Reluctantly, Bill said, "Send him up." His regrets increased as he heard the stomp, thud, stomp, thud movement up the stairs and the approaching steps down the long hall to his bedroom. Bill muttered, "Not another drunk."

Bill escorted the stranger in a black raincoat into his room, noticing his severe limp and his cramped body bent over a cane. The visitor shuffled over to a straight wooden chair opposite the bed and sat down. Then his coat fell open, revealing his Roman collar. "I'm Father Ed Dowling from St. Louis," he said. "A Jesuit friend and I have been struck by the similarity of the AA Twelve Steps and the Spiritual Exercises of St. Ignatius."

"Never heard of them."

Father Dowling laughed and seemed delighted. This endeared him to Bill who found himself looking into the most remarkable eyes he'd ever seen, peering out at him from beneath a soaking lock of pure white hair. Robert Thomsen tells the story in *Bill W.* this way:

> Then the curious little man went on and on, and as he did, Bill could feel his body relaxing, his spirits rising. Gradually he realized that this man sitting across from him was radiating a kind of grace that was filling the room with a strange, indefinable sense of presence. Primarily, Father Ed wanted to talk about the paradox of A.A., the "regeneration," he called it, the strength arising out of total defeat and weakness, the loss of one's old life as a condition for achieving a new one. And Bill nodded, agreed with everything he said...but Bill never really had any words for what he found that night.[4]

Soon Bill was talking about all the AA steps and taking his Fifth Step (telling of the exact nature of his wrongs) with this priest, who with no warning, had limped in from a storm.[5] He told Father Ed about his anger, his impatience, his mounting dissatisfactions: his demands on the world. Father Ed quoted to him, "Blessed are they who hunger and thirst."

When Bill asked whether there was ever to be any satisfaction, the older man snapped back, "Never. Never any." Bill was to be a person who would keep on reaching. In his reaching he would find God's goals, hidden in his own heart.

Bill had made a decision, Father Ed reminded him, to turn his life and his will over to the care of God, and having done this, he was not now to sit in judgment on how he or the world was proceeding. He had only to keep the channels open — and be grateful, of course; it was not up to him to decide how fast or how slowly AA developed. He had only to accept. For whether the two of them liked it or not, the world was undoubtedly proceeding as it should, in God's good time.[6]

Soon they were speaking of conversion and faith, and Father Ed was again quoting Bill's words back to him. No one among them had been able to maintain anything like perfect adherence to these principles.... *They were not saints.... The point was that they were willing to grow along spiritual lines.... They claimed spiritual progress rather than spiritual perfection.*

Before Father Dowling left he pulled his crippled body up and, leaning on his heavy stick, thrust his head forward and looked straight into Bill's eyes. He said there was a force in Bill that was all his own, that had never been on this earth before, and if he did anything to mar it, or block it, it would never exist anywhere again.

That night, for the first time in months, Bill Wilson slept soundly.

CHAPTER 2

Bill's Story

How did this Irish Catholic Jesuit priest come to seek Bill out and become his "spiritual adviser"? Bill told a story in the Big Book about the problems he had with ministers and organized religion.

Near the end of that bleak November [1934], I sat drinking in my kitchen. With a certain satisfaction I reflected there was enough gin concealed about the house to carry me through that night and the next day. My wife was at work. I wondered whether I dared hide a full bottle of gin near the head of our bed. I would need it before daylight.

My musing was interrupted by the telephone. The cheery voice of an old school friend [Ebby Thatcher] asked if he might come over. *He was sober.* It was years since I could remember his coming to New York in that condition. I was amazed. Rumor had it that he had been committed for alcoholic insanity. I wondered how he had escaped. Of course he would have dinner, and then I could drink openly with him....

The door opened and he stood there, looking fresh-skinned and glowing. He refused the drink I pushed across the table.

Simply, but smilingly, he said, "I've got religion."

As Ebby told his conversion story, Bill reflected on ministers: "When they talked of a God personal to me who was love, superhuman strength and direction, I became irritated and my mind snapped shut against such a theory."[7] Great wonder it was that he, Bill Wilson, a Vermont Yankee, could meet Father Ed, a St. Louis Irish Catholic Jesuit priest and his mind did not snap shut.

What brought Bill to this meeting and this friendship? Bill had been a baseball pitcher at Norwich Academy; Father Ed, a catcher in a South Dakota minor league. Sports never brought them together. Both were intensely interested in the skills of democracy. Father Ed was a lifelong member of a group urging democracy through proportional representation.[8] Bill grew up with his grandfather Fayette's democratic dreams. His grandfather fought in the Civil War at the Battle of Gettysburg in July of 1863 and shared with thirteen-year-old Bill his vision: "The idea of democracy... was that all men are equal and that the things they have in common, that hold them together, are stronger than anything that tries to separate them."[9]

Neither sports nor democracy led these two men to meet; suffering introduced them to each other. Father Ed had heard of AA from a former student in Chicago and took the train there to attend several AA meetings. After the Chicago trip, he wrote to the New York AA Office for material, including a Big Book. Then he took the train to New York to meet Bill.

After Father Ed's death in 1960, Bill kept three things of Father Ed's in his Bedford Hills studio: his cane to the right of the fireplace, his crucifix on the wall above the cane; and The Spiritual Exercises of St. Ignatius on a shelf above the window to the left of his desk. The cane (which is still there) speaks of suffering in Father Ed's body, a spine turned to stone from arthritis; the crucifix speaks of his way to cope; The Spiritual Exercises speak of humility and discernment.[10]

All three celebrated a man who lived with suffering. In a July 21, 1952 letter, Bill wrote to Marion, a friend suffering from depression:

> I have learned to be thankful for it (suffering), but at
> the time I certainly wasn't. While I've appreciated the

lessons of suffering after the suffering was over, I never have been able to fully welcome and enjoy it while it was in progress. That's the difference between folks like us and Father Ed. I suppose the ability to always welcome suffering is the hallmark of all things. And I absolutely agree that man certainly is one. In spiritual stature, he towers over all people in my pretty large acquaintance.

Suffering came early in Bill's life. One night Bill's father had been drinking and arguing with his mother. Then he deserted Bill, nine years old at the time, and his sister Dorothy, and his mother. Bill told the story this way:

> Mother took Dorothy and me on what we thought was to be a picnic at beautiful North Dorset Pond, now called Emerald Lake. We sat on the southwest shore under a shade tree, and Mother seemed very quiet, and I think we both had a sense of foreboding.
>
> Then it was that Mother told us that Father had gone for good. To this day, I shiver every time I recall that scene on the grass by the lakefront. It was an agonizing experience for one who apparently had the emotional sensitivity that I did. I hid the wound, however, and never talked about it with anybody, even my sister.[11]

After his parents' divorce, Bill was placed with his maternal grandparents. His mother left to study osteopathy in Boston. He would later interpret the event this way: "And that meant if only [my] parents had loved [me] more, they wouldn't have separated. If [I] had been more lovable, it never would have happened. It always came around to that. It was, it *had* to be, [my] fault. [I] was the guilty one."[12] There was something wrong with him. AA's official history, *Pass It On*, concluded:

> For young Bill, the divorce must have been painful beyond imagining. He was being separated from a father he adored, at a difficult time in the life of a young boy —

the beginning of puberty. To compound the injury, divorce in a small New England town at the beginning of the century — 1906 — was virtually unheard-of; it may have aroused feelings of shame and disgrace that the child of divorced parents today would not understand or share. Bill said he remained depressed for almost a year following his parents' divorce.[13]

Bill decided he would show the town he was "somebody." He lacked anyone or anything to turn to except books and his grandfather Fayette, who had taunted the young Bill, "It's an odd thing: I've been reading a good deal about Australia lately and no one seems to know why Australians are the only people in the world who can make a boomerang."

After almost a year of experimenting, Bill made his final boomerang out of the headboard from his bed. It worked. His grandfather kept repeating, "The very first American to do it, our Willie. The Number One man."

In 1909 Bill traveled from East Dorset to Manchester by train to begin high school at Burr and Burton, a coeducational institution. In a 1955 talk, Bill looked back on this time at the Burr and Burton Academy:

> In that early period I had to be an athlete because I was not an athlete. I had to be a musician because I could not carry a tune. I had to be the president of my class in boarding school. I had to be first in everything because in my perverse heart I felt myself the least of God's creatures. I could not accept this deep sense of inferiority, and so I did become captain of the baseball team, and I did learn to play the fiddle well enough to lead the highschool orchestra, even though it was a terribly bad band. I was the leader and lead I must — or else. So it went. All or nothing. I must be Number One.[14]

At Burr and Burton Academy he became Number One and found this new security.

During the summers Bill worked with Mark Whalon, who

was nine years older than he. They had become friends while string-
ing the first telephone lines into East Dorset. Mark became a "sort
of uncle/father." They hunted and fished together and shared an
interest in Vermont history.

Mark taught Bill about the social ladder in East Dorset. With
Mark, Bill visited his first pub and — with the men and the cider —
Bill felt he was "somebody." Back at school he began again by
dint of hard work to feel that he was important. But then something happened to shake his security.

> I felt secure with grandfather's liberal allowance and
> the love and respect of my schoolmates. I was some-
> body, substantial and real, and lacked only one ingredi-
> ent: romance. Then came the minister's daughter (Ber-
> tha), and in spite of my awkward adolescence things
> were complete. I had romance, security, and applause.
> I was ecstatically happy.
>
> Then one morning the school principal appeared
> with a sad face and announced that my girl had died
> suddenly the night before. I dropped into a depression
> that lasted for three solid years. I did not graduate from
> school. I was unable to finish because I could not accept
> the loss of any part of what I thought belonged to me.[15]

The depression over Bertha's death affected nearly everything. He commented, "Interest in everything except the fiddle
collapsed. No athletics, no schoolwork done, no attention to anyone. I was utterly, deeply, and compulsively miserable, convinced
that my whole life had utterly collapsed." Bill added later, "The
healthy kid would have felt badly, but he would never have sunk
so deep or stayed submerged for so long."[16]

In a 1958 essay, "The Next Frontier — Emotional Sobriety,"
Bill said his basic flaw was "dependence — almost absolute dependence — on people or circumstances to supply me with prestige, security, and the like. Failing to get these things according to
my perfectionist dreams and specifications, I had fought for them.
And when defeat came, so did my depression." In this article,
written when Bill was sixty-three, he reflected, "Those adolescent

urges so many of us have for top approval, perfect security and perfect romance — urges quite appropriate to age seventeen — prove to be an impossible way of life when we are at age forty-seven or fifty-seven. I've taken immense wallops in all these areas because of my failure to grow up emotionally and spiritually." Again, in the same article, looking back from the vantage of later life, Bill sees this wanting to be secure through approval and romance as what kept him stuck in depression for ten years.[17]

In 1914 at age nineteen he visited his father, who was living in British Columbia. His father was more interested in his new wife than in Bill. Bill left depressed. He began study at Norwich Military Academy. During the next summer at Emerald Lake Bill met Lois Burnham. He said later, "She lifted me out of this despond [Bill's word], and we fell very deeply in love, and I was cured temporarily, because now I loved and was loved, and there was hope again." Bill adds, "At the unconscious level, I have no doubt she was already becoming my mother, and I haven't any question that that was a very heavy component in her interest in me. I think Lois came along and picked me up as tenderly as a mother does a child."[18]

As the United States was drawn into World War I, Bill became a second lieutenant in the coast artillery. At society parties to cover inadequacy he began to drink. He married Lois in her family's Swedenborgian Church on January 24, 1918. Overseas, he continued to find a place for himself as a natural leader of men. He also continued to drink, adding brandy and wine.

In England an epidemic kept Bill and his regiment detained at a camp near Winchester. Bill, anxious about what lay ahead in the war, visited Winchester Cathedral. While inside, he was taken by a sort of ecstasy, stirred by a "tremendous sense of presence." "I have been in many cathedrals since, and have never experienced anything like it. For a brief moment, I had needed and wanted God. There had been a humble willingness to have Him with me — and He came." Things, he felt, would be all right.[19]

On his discharge from the army in May 1919, he settled in Brooklyn with Lois and took a series of odd jobs and night courses at Brooklyn Law School. He began investigating companies for brokerage firms. He continued drinking. Lois suffered through three ectopic pregnancies and the surgical removal of her ovaries, a tragedy for both Bill and Lois. They tried to adopt, but a friend had warned the adoption agency of Bill's drinking. Lois remarked later, "...after all hope of having children had died, his bouts with alcohol had become even more frequent."[20]

In the 1929 stock market crash, Bill lost his job and found himself $60,000 in debt. A Montreal firm picked him up and gave him a job until he had to be fired because of his drinking and some fighting at a country club. Drinking again, he missed the funeral of Lois's mother. Lois now had to work at Macy's to support them both.

Between 1933 and 1934, he was hospitalized four times at Charles B. Towns Hospital, a drying-out facility for alcoholics in Manhattan, Central Park West. He experienced the shakes, DTs, and thoughts of suicide. In November 1934 (as mentioned at the start of this chapter), his friend Ebby visited him and offered him some hope. A sober and serene Ebby talked of religion and the need for a power greater than himself, and he introduced Bill to the Oxford Group.[21]

Later, after a three-day drunk, Bill checked himself into Towns Hospital again on December 11, 1934. Ebby visited him on the second or third evening and explained the principles of the Oxford Group. During the night, Bill cried out, "If there is a God, let Him show himself." The room became filled with light, peace — God. Dr. William Duncan Silkworth on the next day confirmed the experience as spiritual.[22] Ebby brought Bill a copy of William James's *The Varieties of Religious Experience*, and Bill was struck by James saying, "the common denominator of spiritual experience is pain and utter hopelessness." In other words, deflation at depth.[23]

Later Dr. Silkworth helped Bill (who was now trying to sober up other drunks) by telling him to drop preaching at alcoholics and just share *his* story. Bill began at this time to talk about alcoholism as "an obsession of the mind coupled to increasing physical sensitivity," Silkworth's "allergy theory."

In May of 1935 Bill went to Akron, Ohio, on a business deal. The deal failed; he wanted to drink. Instead he phoned a minister, Dr. Tunks, who suggested he call Henrietta Seiberling. She invited him to her home and asked Dr. Bob Smith, another alcoholic still drinking, over to talk with Bill. AA begins in their mutual vulnerability and honesty, the telling of their stories after Dr. Bob's last drunk on June 10, 1935. To keep their own sobriety, Bill and Bob began to tell their story to those who were still suffering and in St. Thomas Hospital. They told their stories to Bill D., an attorney, who had DTs and had blackened the eye of the nurse who had put him in the Akron City Hospital the night before. After listening to Bill's and Dr. Bob's stories, he became the third man. Five years later brings us to the meeting of Bill W. and Father Ed described in Chapter One. Suffering gathered men together, one by one, into a ballpark called AA.

The suffering of others brought Father Ed to Bill. Yet in Father Ed's case, was it only the suffering *outside* himself that led him up those steps of the 24th Street clubhouse? What was the story of Father Dowling's life? Did Father Ed experience suffering and deflation at depth as did Bill and Dr. Bob?

CHAPTER 3

Father Ed's Story

Edward Patrick Dowling was born September 1, 1898, in a section
of St. Louis known as Baden. In later life Father Ed would joke
that this area, north of St. Louis, by the Mississippi River held
"the brains and health of the city." The people in the "booby traps,"
the ring of suburbs around the heart of the city, Dowling deplored
as not "having an alert wide-awake thought in years." He later
mounted a map on his office wall with pins outlining the ring of
suburbs that he called the "booby trap."[24]

His grandfather was the lineal descendant of Farrell Dowling,
a forthright Irishman, exiled by Cromwell to Connaught — the Irish
Siberia — in 1654 because of his candor.[25] This grandfather came
to America from the Irish potato famine just before the Civil War
and started a railroad construction company in north St. Louis.
Ed's own father managed the property. His mother was Anastasia
Cullinane from another Irish family. Her folks ran a livery and an
undertaking parlor. The Cullinane men were active in St. Louis
politics and played on local soccer and baseball teams — common
sports for those who lived in Baden, settled mostly by Germans.
Their school, Holy Cross, had classes in German. The Dowlings
sent Ed to Holy Name School as soon as he was old enough to take
the streetcar. Later, the Irish in Baden started Mount Carmel parish.

Both parents were religious. His mother attended 8 A.M. mass
every morning. Often men seeking meals would appear at their

back door where they knew the Dowlings would share their supper and a room in the basement for an overnight.[26] Ed was the oldest child and the big brother to four younger children. Anna, who was three years younger, never married and would later become Ed's secretary. James, two years younger than Anna, died at age fifteen of influenza while a student at St. Mary's College in Kansas. Mary, four years younger than James, would become a Religious of the Sacred Heart and librarian at Maryville College. She and Anna would later establish the Dowling Archives at Maryville's new campus in memory of Father Ed. The fifth child, Paul, who was born two years after Mary, entered the Jesuit novitiate, but did not stay. Later, he became a newspaper reporter and married Beatrice Murphy in 1939. They had two children, Paul and Mary.

Ed grew up playing sandlot baseball. After Holy Name Grade School and three years at St. Louis University High School, he went on to St. Mary's College in Kansas, the school of his father and grandfather. During his two years there, he became captain and catcher for the baseball team. He barnstormed in the summer of 1916 as a semi-pro ball player (catcher) and had a tryout with the Boston Red Sox and later with the St. Louis Browns. Neither team gave him a contract. He took a job as a reporter for ten dollars a week with the *St. Louis Globe Democrat*. This began his lifelong interest in news, government, and politics. World War I called him away for six months as a private. After the war, he returned as a reporter to the *Globe*.

In 1919 after an all-night party at a bar with other reporters, he entered the Jesuits at St. Stanislaus Novitiate in Florissant, Missouri, wearing white duck pants with his favorite red-and-white-striped silk shirt. He carried no bags, only another pair of white duck pants wrapped in newspaper under his arm. A week later he saw someone polishing the wood floors with his silk shirt. He did not expect to stay. His reporter friends never expected him to stay. But stay he did — even when novitiate life became a desert devoid of belief.

In his second year of novitiate, he faced a major crisis of faith and had to give up the God who made no demands. God ceased to let him be "comfortable." This began his Gethsemene, a two-year period of intense spiritual suffering. Years later in an April 18, 1944, talk he referred to this experience of "bottoming out" as a young Jesuit.

> But here tonight, I am discussing a problem to which I am not entirely alien. Up to the age of 21 my spirituality, my religion, my faith was a comfortable, unchallenged nursery habit. Then over a course of some months, the most important months of my life saw that faith, that religion, drift away. It began to make demands. And as it ceased to be comfortable and comforting to big and important I, when it ceased to "yes" my body and soul, I found that I moved away from it. I am not utterly unacquainted with atheism. I know and respect agnosticism and I have been a bed-fellow with spiritual confusion, not merely the honest and sincere kind, but the self-kidding kind.[27]

Later, he told others the cure he found in these words, "Dwell in my way and you will know the truth." About the same time of his Jesuit training at Florissant during a walk along the Missouri River, he started feeling a twinge in one of his legs. Upon checking with a doctor, he found he had incurable arthritis. When he was thirty, his spine — in his words — would "turn to stone." He added, "I yield in my stiffness to no one." He would develop an attitude to deal with his suffering that he called "Glad Gethsemene." Later that would be key to his understanding of AA's Steps Six and Seven.[28]

After studying philosophy in St. Louis and teaching in Chicago at Ignatius High School, each for three years, Dowling returned to St. Mary's College in Kansas to study theology. Father Moran, his superior for his three years of teaching at Loyola, wrote this evaluation.

> He is trustworthy, generally dependable and a very honest character. He is conscientious in his work, thinks clearly, logically, and has business ability above average. He would succeed very well in an executive position.

He is ambitious, wants to get ahead, and possesses a good deal of shrewdness in getting what he wants from people and from circumstances.

Though possessing some aggressiveness, a lot of physical energy, will power and firmness, he is apt to procrastinate at times and to excuse himself on practical grounds for small lapses in conduct, though he is in no sense dishonest or hypocritical. He is modest and reticent about his own affairs. He has a very good physique and constitution. He is fond of outdoor sports — probably has played them a good deal.

He is gifted along scientific lines rather than artistic and literary lines. He has a comparatively weak imagination, though he shows some constructive ability. He has a gift for mathematics. He is eccentric and has a very distinctive and original personality. He is careless about small things, and is very absent-minded. He is self-conscious at times and somewhat sensitive. He is a man of simple tastes, though he has some strong likes and dislikes. He is generous, friendly, humble and modest.[29]

Father Moran caught Dowling well but missed his wild imagination. After three years of teaching high school, Dowling went to St. Marys, Kansas, to study theology for four years. Father Moran's letter served as the standard letter to the Jesuit provincial staff, who needed a confirmation that Dowling was ready after his three-year teaching experiment to begin the study of theology and preparation for the priesthood.

At that time the atmosphere of Jesuit training was highly intellectual and competitive. Jesuits were divided into two groups: the long and short course or "the leapers and the creepers."[30] Many Jesuits were hoping to go on after theology to study for doctorates and teach at places like St. Louis University. At that time some young Jesuits felt the long course and a Ph.D. was the way to arrive. Father Dan Lord, who would later be Father Ed's boss at The Queen's Work, reflected on his own ambivalent feelings around his lack of a Ph.D.

I would be less than honest if I did not confess I would like Ph.D. after my name. The honorary degrees are kind, but I do not feel that I have rated or earned them. A Ph.D. means long and laborious years of grinding work. Certainly I would like to know that years of advanced and graduate studies would have added to my store of knowledge. I would like the tools with which the Doctor of Philosophy has been equipped.

It embarrasses me to realize that for the second half of my life, I would not have been welcomed on most Jesuit university faculties. Yet I am not sure of what higher education might have done to me.[31]

Lord's words caught the ambivalence: the higher degree would be a ticket into the university level, but who needed it? This quote shows the outsider, looking in on the university world. Father Ed would describe St. Louis University as the place where "he did his laundry." By choice, Father Ed would also be an outsider, judged by the insiders. Father Dan Lord would choose him to work as his public relations man for The Queen's Work (a Catholic publishing group) and coordinator of The Summer School of Catholic Action, a traveling summer school moving through major cities for Catholic high school students.

Father Ed, in the long course until his second year of theology, flunked the Latin oral exam thesis on whether angels had bodies. Both the rector and the provincial reprimanded him for spending too much time on a bulletin board with news items and not enough time on his theology. He wrote to both that he had learned much from this exchange, listed how much time he spent on theology, and added frankly that the thesis was a footnote and not really covered in class. The bulletin board took little time; he merely put up news items others had received in their mail. With both men he was respectful and direct.

Later, some Jesuits would consider him a disorganized, intellectual lightweight. One Jesuit joked that if Dowling had a purgatory, it would be finishing his incomplete sentences. A good friend and theology teacher at St. Louis University, Father Ben Fulkerson, said of him, "Dowling was a kind of knave in the king's court. He would grunt. But he was smarter than all the king's councilors. His manners and ways of expressing himself went against him. He seemed disorganized, a bit slap-happy, a roughneck." Fulkerson told the story that once Father Ed paid a visit to St. Ignatius High School in Chicago. The young Jesuit who opened the door for Father Ed left him in the front parlor and said to another companion, "Who is this funny-looking guy?"[32] Within minutes reporters from all the Chicago papers were taking down Father Ed's every word.

Under this unlikely exterior, Father Dan Lord of The Queen's Work must have spotted Father Ed's gifts. He chose him as a writer, public relations person, and a speaker in the Summer School of Catholic Action. Father Ed would be at The Queen's Work from 1931 until his death in 1960. A reporter friend, Sam Lambert, claimed this job was a cover-up for his real job, being "God's ambassador to humanity." Sam also summed up the judgment of Father Ed's closest friends: "Father Ed was a genius whose specialty was suffering: his own, that of those who sought his help, and that of Christ, especially in the Garden of Gethsemene."[33]

Father Barnaby Faherty, a Jesuit who worked with Dowling at The Queen's Work, commented on Dowling's highly personal style: "Dowling's brilliance was intuitive, unstructured and directed to the deep experience of human need."[34] Neither quality would have been captured in a Latin oral exam on the corporeality of angels.

Not only did he experience the suffering from his arthritis and the judgments of fellow Jesuits, but also from his own compulsive smoking and overeating. In 1944 his St. Louis AA friends asked him to stop smoking. By using the Twelve Steps, he did stop. He wrote Bill, "I've stopped smoking, but I am becoming as fat as a hog." Twice friends saw him finish in one sitting a quarter pound of butter and box of saltines. Late one night, he ate all the strawberries for the entire Jesuit community and became so sick he had to receive the last rites. He wrote a friend, "I have been anointed twice for gluttony. After that the rest is a curtain call. My high was 242 pounds. Treating appetizing foods as an alcoholic should treat alcohol, I now weigh about 167. The greatest help I have received on diet is the recognition that I react to certain foods the way an alcoholic reacts to alcohol and that the road to sanity is through pretty severe abstinence."[35] No stranger to addiction and compulsion, he would joke to Bill and Lois that they needed to start a group called "obese obvious" for him and "nicotine nobodies" for Bill. Both compulsions hastened the deaths of two fine men.

Another Jesuit, Father James McQuade, who worked with Father Ed, said Father Ed had a sense of humor about himself that enabled his Jesuit community to joke with him about his compulsive eating. They accused him of "eating his diet first, and then having his regular meal."[36]

Mary Wehner, a worker at The Queen's Work, wrote about Father Ed at a staff buffet dinner there.

> I happened to be standing next to him (Father Ed) at the buffet table watching a group square dancing. As we stood there completely absorbed, Father Ed would take a piece of bread, slap a piece of ham on it, fold it over and gulp it down. This happened several times, maybe five or six. I said, knowing he was notorious for being oblivious to what he ate, "Oh, Father, why don't you let me get you some decent food?"
>
> "No, thanks, dear, I'm on a strict diet."[37]

Later, Father Ed would be hospitalized for eye, weight, and heart problems at St. John's Hospital. Some say Bill had the 1955 AA convention in St. Louis because of Father Ed's failing health. At one point, Father Ed wrote a letter to Bill that he was experiencing depression from medication for high blood pressure. Bill, who had battled depression for ten years, wrote on this letter of Father Ed's as he filed it, "dear man."

Other Jesuits recall stories. Father Larry Chuminatto, who directed the White House Retreat Center outside St. Louis, said he once dropped into Father Ed's office to consult with him on some matter. After they were done, Father Ed started to look around and then leaned over with some difficulty from his chair next to his desk and drew out of the middle drawer a six-shooter. He aimed it at the ceiling and fired it two times. Two loud bangs from the cap gun went off. In a few seconds a young woman appeared at the door. Father Ed asked her to bring in some items. He then turned to Father Chuminatto and said, "The buzzer is broken, so we are using the gun for a while."[38]

Father Ed never ceased trying to find the right structure to help people: AA; Cana; Recovery Inc.; groups for those suffering from scruples. Mary Wehner remembered this story:

> One day I was called up to his office along with Richard Marty, a young innocent lad from the shipping room. Since Father Ed was also famous for his matchmaking, when Richard and I met outside his office door, we both had the same thought: "I hope he isn't going to try to promote a match between us." At the thought of this Richard's face became brick red.
>
> He wanted to promote a match all right, but not the kind of match we had thought. Ed had many friends among newspaper men and especially among the sports writers. Through one of them he had been out to the old Cardinal Park, Sportsmen's Park for a ballgame the night before. "Baseball," he told us, "wastes more time than any other sport. Last night I took a stop watch out and timed the minutes they wasted winding up, fouling off pitches, etc. I am going to write some new rules and I want you and Richard to each get up a team to see if they will work. Then I am going to send the results to the commissioner." What a sigh of relief we breathed when we realized this was the only match he had in mind.[39]

Without the help of Mary and Richard, the new rules were tested. Father Jim Swetnan wrote about his most interesting encounter with Father Ed. In the spring of 1950, Swetnan was in charge of organizing athletic programs for the Jesuits in philosophy training. These Jesuits used to take their bus to Forest Park for games of softball or soccer. TV had just started to cover baseball. Father Ed had an idea what would make the coverage better and approached Jim. "I hear you are in charge of the athletic program."

"Yes, Father."

"I want you to organize a special game of softball for me."

He thought the rules of baseball/softball should be modified for more pleasant television viewing. The infield was to be oval-shaped so the TV camera could take in everything without swiveling back and forth.[40] The count was to be reduced to two strikes and three balls. Swetnan organized the two teams and Father Ed explained what he wanted. The men caught on right away and entered into the spirit of the new game. They played for over an hour and had a good time. The score was up in the dozens of runs. Father Ed, who had been quite a baseball player in his day, sat on the sidelines, chuckling. At the end he pronounced himself satisfied and took his place on the bus. Midway back to St. Louis University he announced, "Thou shalt not muzzle the ox," and instructed the bus driver to stop at a drive-in, where he treated the men to ice cream cones.[41]

Dowling came alive whenever he found the right structure to help people: in this case, baseball.[42] He would later bring Recovery Inc. to St. Louis for the emotionally disturbed, a Montserrat group for those suffering from scruples, Cana for married couples, Divorcees Anonymous for those recovering from "failed marriages," and AA for those suffering from alcoholism.

Another story told how Father Ed used to travel from his living space at St. Louis University several miles south on Grand to his Queen's Work office. He would stand out in the middle of the street and blow a whistle. Esta Jones, who worked in the emergency room at St. John's Hospital, said that she once saw Father Ed come to the Queen's Work in the mayor's limousine with chauffeur. The next time she saw him, he was alighting from a garbage truck. In her words, "He'd had a good time on both rides." Cab drivers in the Melbourne Hotel area knew his whistle and competed to drive him down Grand. Along the way, he would ask the driver to stop for others.

John G. Scott, a cousin to Father Ed, said that Father Ed had the gift of being present to a person and finding what that person needed. Often this one-on-one meeting would lead to the person joining a group. One lady recalled that when her marriage was on the rocks, Father Ed was there and got her to the right group, a group called 7UP for parents who had more than seven children.[43] Her marriage survived.

This is the Jesuit who took the train to meet Bill W. in New York, a Jesuit committed to obedience and authority, but at the same time a passionate lover of democracy and the grassroots power of people with the same wounds to heal each other. After that New York 1940 meeting between Bill W. and Father Ed, there would be a new story, about the power of two men who became friends. That story appears in their letters.

CHAPTER 4

The Story in Letters 1941 to 1944

The two men had met on a sleet-filled November night in 1940. However, it wasn't until New Year's of 1942 that they formally got together, when Bill invited Father Ed to his home. Father Ed wrote Bill on January 6, 1942, "I want to thank Lois for seconding your efforts to make that New Year's day one of the happiest I've ever spent." In a later letter Dowling wrote, "I often recall our New Year's together just after Pearl Harbor."[44]

That New Year's they talked of Bill's interest in psychic phenomena. Their first letters were about voices from the other world. Bill had found God in his conversion experience at Towns Hospital; would psychic experience, he asked, satisfy his thirst for God and be *from God?*[45] Father Ed, responding to Bill's interest, wrote:

> Since talking to you, I've been asking some questions that surprise me a little about the prevalence of the phenomena. I am expecting in the mail, a photograph that I saw in Washington depicting the face of Christ in a rainbow. The woman who pointed the camera — so the story goes — at the rainbow, swooned at the sight in the camera finder. Even when the film was developed, her husband could not see it until it was pointed out. I am struck by the face. I just mention this as one of the three instances that have developed from my casual inquiries.[46]

Then Father Ed suggested two books and consultation with a New York Jesuit and dear friend, Father La Buffe.[47]

Bill sought light from Father Ed as he plunged into the darkness of the psychic world. How does a person discern voices from the other side? Is it the voice of God or an evil spirit? Will the voice lead to death or life?

Underneath this is another question: how to choose the next life-giving step in recovery. Solid choices presuppose skill in discerning from one's center between voices and choices that lead to life. For these choices, Father Ed and Bill will repeat this pattern: *listening, discerning, choosing,* as both seek to know God's plan for them and AA.[48]

Bill found in Father Ed a port in the storm of early AA difficulties. Bill could pull in, think out loud, and discern which way to sail. He wrote to Father Ed on February 3, 1942:

> Thank you very much for your visit to us. All who have come to know you a little want to know you better. We who saw you — more than a little — are fortunate. I wonder if you can realize how you have opened our minds — how you exemplify to some of us those qualities of humility, discipline, patience, and devotion — about which we AA's talk a lot but do too little. Everyone can feel that you practice the presence of God and that is so much better than preaching. I'm saying these things because it may be helpful to you if you know how some of us feel. Besides, it's a pleasure to express one's feelings fully when one knows he will not be misunderstood.

Bill concluded the letter by noting a small incident of Dowling, as the sponsor at work. "When you were here, you found me on what AA's call a dry bender— you snapped me out of it in a hurry, *that second step* (but you mustn't take these occurrences too seriously either, for some of the time *I do try* to think and talk sense), I do thank God for my many blessings and know that of myself I am nothing without Him."[49]

In this last paragraph Bill turned again to Dowling as sponsor and gave him permission to admonish him if he deluded himself.

It is a firm principle with most of us that *as far as AA goes,* each member has the absolute right to seek God as he will. Sometimes, contemplation of that principle gives rise to the thought that we are still free to think and act as we like, provided we are in pursuit of the truth. Which (lofty?) notion can be rationalized by a child like me into a neat device by which I may do as I damn please — and am perfectly justified all the while! I'm sure I know not much yet of obedience, so please rap my knuckles when you think I need it.

In the postscript Bill asked Father Ed whether he would and could be a trustee for the Alcoholic Foundation. Dowling wrote his provincial superior on the issue, citing the way he saw his gift to AA: sharing the discernment principles of the second week of *The Spiritual Exercises of St. Ignatius,* which involved choosing the best over the less good. This implied subtle discernment both between the good and the better, and tracing where an inner movement is headed: death or life.[50]

Father Ed, in a letter of February 18, 1942, told Bill he was waiting for his provincial to decide on an AA trusteeship.

The prestige and the flattering social value of it makes me want it. The feeling that any pronounced institutional bias in the "officialdom" of AA might minimize the usefulness and frighten timid agnostics is a strong reason in my mind for its inadvisability. You must not forget the sinister suspicions that would be created by the presence of a cross-back, mackerel-snapping Jesuit near the cash register. I am afraid it would produce an epidemic of dry benders and spiritual shakes. However, I will feel safer in my decision if it is guided by obedience. I will let you know if Father Provincial decided to make an exception to a general policy of not undertaking trusteeships involving dispositions of money.

The answer finally came: "No. It should be a bishop to relate to AA." This "no" left Father Ed freer to relate to Bill and AA as friend and spiritual sponsor. Dowling as spiritual sponsor would prove a greater gift than Dowling as trustee. Here both men honored spiritual accountability: Bill in listening both to Dowling as sponsor and AA as "group conscience."[51] Dowling's accountability was in his openness with Father Dan Lord, his local superior, and with his provincial in both cases through his vow of obedience. Dowling too, opened his soul to his spiritual director or soul friend, Father Dismas Clark.[52]

Then Father Ed named an AA grace now in his blood: "In the confusion of World War II, the AA personality is keeping an easy pace, convinced that somehow, some time, the cockeyed world will land on its feet. I am grateful to God for the AA virus in my spiritual blood stream."[53]

He concluded with a reference to *America,* a weekly magazine published by the Jesuits. They "had an article on AA last week. Haven't had a chance to read it though my impression is that the writer, while sympathetic, was guided by written material rather than personal contact."[54] Dowling was working the steps himself, enough to have caught "the AA virus," and was no longer a spectator but practitioner and defender of AA, especially in Catholic circles. Much like Bill, the Yankee pragmatist, he affirmed that we only really know *by doing.*

"That spiritual essence you radiate travels even over the telephone," Bill wrote on May 25, 1942. "So Smith and I were grateful for even the sniff you blew us. Speaking of Smith, I wish you knew him better. But that is a long job. Like all Vermont Yankees he has inhibitions. Seemingly, he has developed spiritually by hanging on to them while I, who have lost some of mine, continue to get more sinful in proportion!"[55]

Then Bill moves on to his discernment issue: what to do about joining the army. Bill reports:

> Still struggling to get in the army. No luck yet. Maybe I'm supposed to be a missionary after all. I wish I knew. Suppose it's all a question of opening up channels and waiting for an indication. There is a feeling somehow that in any event this year will be a steadier one, and in no small part, thanks to you. Less oscillating between the spiritual jag and dry bender.

Again, Bill affirmed Father Ed as a person who helped him keep steady through the ups and downs of dry benders as Bill opened up another discernment issue: how to choose about going into the army. He had served in World War I, he wanted very much to rejoin in World War II. Discernment for Bill was, "to open up all channels and wait for an indication." The United States was at war with Germany, Italy, and Japan. Bill had been raised in a tradition of military service. Now at forty-seven he was deeply concerned over the war and wanted to enlist. He charted the daily progress of the war with pushpins on a wall map in his office. But after his army physical, Bill's ulcers earned him rejection from the army. His age and his desire to be reinstated as an officer also may not have helped his cause.

Bill went so far as to write the head of Selective Service and suggest that recovering alcoholics in AA should not be rejected and that they could handle the stress of war without drinking. The response of the army was that "It would be manifestly unwise to subject these men, who have apparently made a satisfactory adjustment in their individual environment, [to] one where stress and strain play an important part and where the temptation to resort to their former inclinations would be far more inviting."[56]

Part of discernment involves working with reality as it is unfolding. A person doesn't discern well unless he can explore options or as Bill puts it, "keep his channels open." Bill is learning both discernment and acceptance of nos: no army and no Father Ed as trustee.

Father Ed in his next letter (May 27, 1942) responded to an article Bill sent him:

> The *Ecclesiastical Review* by Father O'Connor pains me on a couple of scores. It seems to be written without observation of personal reactions to AA. He says that "to appeal to a man's religious sense but not interfere with his belief is a distinction too fine for practical experiment." This would seem to rule out judicial oaths. I am tempted to write to Father O'Connor. My observation is Catholics are in vastly worse spiritual danger in drinking than they are in AA. Over and above this

relative improvement, AA contains positive confirmations of Catholic beliefs and practices that most of the Catholic AA's had tended to abandon.

Here Father Ed was beginning to show his role as ambassador-interpreter between AA and the Catholic church. He would clarify the scope of AA to priests and bishops around issues like the use of the term "higher power." Later Bill asked him to write a one-page appendix for the Big Book which would in effect serve as a working sign of Church approval for those Catholics who needed this.[57]

In the same letter Father Ed mentioned that he had now met the co-founder, Dr. Robert Smith, on his own turf, Akron.

Doc Smith is so real and I would feel bad if I didn't have a well grounded hope of coming to know him better. In our Akron talk, Smith seemed to have a sincere respect for the Jesuit Order because of its social activities, but he was a bit scandalized at the thought of the Trappist Order which spends most of its life in silence and prayer. I suggested that trafficking with God in prayer is a pretty high society and a very influential social activity — that these people are our lobbyists before the divine legislature.

Father Ed enclosed his summer schedule and asked for addresses of AA meetings in St. Paul and New Orleans. On his travels he used AA meetings as (he would say) his "lonely hearts club." Although Dowling was not an alcoholic, Bill seemed to have some unspoken agreement that Dowling could attend AA meetings as a special friend or "fellow traveler," a common practice in the early days of AA.

The middle section of Dowling's letter spoke to Bill's anxiety about whether or not the army would accept him. "The sense of knowing where we are going, how our next months and years are to be plotted is not only a precious comfort, but it must sometimes beget dependence on God's hand because so often this information seems to be ladled in teaspoonfuls rather than bucketsful." As usual, Dowling framed the specific problem in a larger context; not just the army but the whole of a person's life involved not knowing the future, realizing rather that we are not God, but creatures.

Again, for these two men, this not knowing the next step made more precious whatever hints, wisdom, discernment each could find about God's plan for each other and the whole of AA. In the middle of this letter Father Ed dropped challenges to detachment:

> Most spiritual development seems to be not through achievement but through detachment:
> — Detachment from the sensual gratification of alcohol brings the spiritual gifts of clear thinking and peace of mind.
> — Detachment from the spiritual goal of authorship and proprietorship brings the spiritual gift of fellowship with thousands who could be authors and proprietors.
> — Detachment from the sophisticated satisfaction of seeing one's own way can bring the peace of a childlike dependence on a "father who can't let us down."

Dowling challenged Bill to let go of ego more and more, both for his own peace of mind and for the larger good of AA. Dowling's detachment challenge came at the right moment: Bill would soon begin writing The Twelve Traditions of AA. Detachment would bring humility and peace. This peace would be for Bill a sign of God confirming love that Bill had already experienced at Winchester Cathedral and at Towns Hospital. Peace confirmed Bill in his mission; detachment would serve anonymity and unity.[58]

CHAPTER 5

In Touch on the Run

In less than two years Dowling had become friend and sponsor for Bill Wilson. In this last role Dowling had challenged Bill to listen to the desires ("thirst") as a place where God's plan will be revealed.[59] Bill had become more open about "dry benders" and the voices from the other side. Dowling, as on the first night both men met, again and again called Bill to the first three steps both for himself and for AA as a whole. He calls him to detachment, letting go — a big order, the work of a lifetime.

The next letters catch the two men in touch on the run. Dowling's next letter (July 15, 1942) finds him writing from Minneapolis, one of the cities visited by the Summer School of Catholic Action. In these stops across the country at big city hotels, The Queen's Work staff offered young people talks, discussions, and liturgies. Father Dan Lord directed their singing and dancing in his large musicals.[60] Dowling himself gave talks on social justice, marriage, the family, proportional representation, suffering, AA — whatever his current interest. James McQuade, another Queen's Work Jesuit, described Dowling's speaking style.

> He was a newspaper man and had the mental habits of a columnist. He would speak from current newspaper "clippings," which he would have in his hands in seeming disorder, and all of this "stuff" was spontaneous and bristled with one liners.[61]

Father Ed wrote to Bill from such a gathering in Minneapolis and enclosed the summer school schedule with the suggestion they meet in either New York or Washington, D.C., both cities on the Summer School of Catholic Action tour. Each spring Father Ed sent his schedule to Bill in hopes they could meet in New York when he was at Fordham speaking for the Summer School.

In the same letter he mentioned his custom of visiting AA. "Visited the elaborate club house in Minneapolis after a meeting. They are doing splendidly."[62] He suggested that Bill check with the clerk at the National Press Club in Washington, who would know his whereabouts. Father Ed, on the run, managed to use as his home bases both AA meetings and newspapermen.

In his next letter to Dowling, Bill enclosed a letter (January 21, 1943) from a Father Marcus O'Brien, who had written Bill that Catholics in AA were having trouble with the words, "higher power," and would prefer "God." Bill included his two-page answer to Father O'Brien, mentioning that the Catholic Committee on Publications checked out the Big Book before it was published and that Father Dowling had given the AA movement a favorable review in Queen's Work publications. Again, Father Ed functioned as the ambassador between AA and the "official" Catholic Church.

Bill's last paragraph to Father O'Brien clarified what AA is and is not: "It must never be forgotten that the purpose of Alcoholic Anonymous is to sober up alcoholics. There is no religious or spiritual requirement for membership. No demands are made on anyone. An experience is offered which members may accept or reject. That is up to them." By underlining that AA is not a religion, Bill relieved those good Christians who thought they were competing with another religion. Bill continued to Father Ed:

> As I took the liberty of using your name, I thought you would like to see his letter and my reply. On such questions I feel a little out of my element. Indeed I may be much out of order this time. If so, slap me down! The nicest thing I can think of is that if I am to be slapped by anyone, I'd rather it be you. I see by the papers that people call you "Father Eddie" and that you are a Jesuit of unusual promise. They will be putting you down in

the kitchen if you don't look out! You have no idea
how many times I think of our talks together. To me
they are really treasured experiences.

Dowling replied, "Thanks for the carbon to Father O'Brien.
You understand how I feel and your use of my views in your letter
accurately reflects my sentiments."[63]

In the same letter he suggested that Bill look at Poulain's
Graces of Interior Prayer and "page over the last third of it and
you will recognize some familiar situations, which a good many
Catholics would find strange."[64] Apparently, Dowling wanted to
affirm Bill's strange experience in Towns Hospital as *of God.*[65]
Dowling concluded, "Your reference to the news item saying that
people call me Father Eddie and that I am a Jesuit of unusual
promise had my vanity all atwitter. I usually send out my own
publicity blurbs. I missed that one."

Bill too had been on the move. He and Lois had traveled by
train across the States with stops at major AA cities.[66] These stops
included meals, local sights, and dinner, followed by an AA meeting
where Bill always spoke. Coffee and more conversation followed
the meeting. After a few hours of sleep they had breakfast with
local AAs and more conversation. All the AAs were anxious to
tell Bill their own stories and to hear his.[67]

Bill and Lois returned home January 22, 1944. The tour had
been a success for Bill and the fellowship. What happened next
came as a complete surprise: Bill was plunged into a suicidal
depression that would last until 1955.[68]

CHAPTER SIX

The Purple Haze: Depression

Bill might have thought with his sobriety and the beginnings of AA: clear skies, happy sailing. But he found himself plunged into depression. He began to write to others suffering depression. "Maybe we all can be the spearhead for the next major advance into the dark purple field of neurosis (or is that the color of it?)."[69] His struggle will give hope to others who face — after confronting their major addiction — "just one more" recovery issue.

But all that was to jump into sunshine and slide over the depth of Bill's depression. Bill himself told of how serious his depression was when he described forcing himself just to walk.

> When I was tired and couldn't concentrate, I used to fall back on an affirmation toward life that took the form of simple walking and deep breathing. I sometimes told myself that I couldn't do even this — that I was too weak. But I learned that this was the point at which I could not give in without becoming still more depressed.
>
> So I would set myself a small stint. I would determine to walk a quarter of a mile. And I would concentrate by counting my breathing — say, six steps to each slow inhalation and four to each exhalation. Having done the quarter-mile, I found that I could go on, maybe a half-mile more. Then another half-mile, and maybe another.

This was encouraging. The false sense of physical weakness would leave me (this feeling being so characteristic of depressions). The walking and especially the breathing were powerful affirmations toward life and living and away from failure and death. The counting represented a minimum discipline in concentration, to get some rest from the wear and tear of fear and guilt.[70]

Bill would also push himself to write just half a page for the *Twelve Steps and Twelve Traditions*.[71] The New York AA Archives file of letters Bill wrote to others suffering from depression as he did shows the many ways Bill struggled to climb out of depression. Nell Wing, Bill's secretary, claimed those close to Bill were deeply concerned. She mentioned days when Bill would be dictating to her only to stop and break down, weeping.[72]

He had so much to be thankful for: he had put the cork in the bottle. Why this depression? To another old-timer he wrote, "Many in recovery were going through the same difficulties with depression." Today, many identify with Bill when after facing their primary addiction, they find other compulsions (smoking, eating, sex, etc.) needing attention. Their response: anger. "Oh God, not another!" And for some: depression.

To Ollie, suffering from depression, Bill wrote in a letter of January 4, 1956, "I suppose about half the old-timers have neurotic hangovers of one sort or another. Certainly I can number myself among them."[73] To Harry Jones from Detroit, another person suffering depression, he reflected, "Your personality pattern is ever so much like mine. Maybe we will find how the 12 steps can work in depth."[74] Bill continues in a letter to "Babe" N., "Believe me, I know what you have suffered, and share your joy in getting well. Among older A.A.'s, there is a great deal of this nervous breakdown business. I certainly share your view that glandular ill health plays a heavy part in many of them. I also believe that the withdrawal of alcohol is likely to accentuate the neurosis in many of us. Our neurosis may break out in very aggravated form after a few years of sobriety."[75]

Bill told Nell Wing the cause of his depression might be biochemical. Clearly, he experienced it as manic-depressive, since the most crippling depressions followed periods of intense emotional and physical activity.[76] What made matters even worse, some AA members suggested he just wasn't working the steps "hard enough."

Clearly, Bill and Father Ed found themselves in the ballpark of suffering: Bill from depression, Father Ed from arthritis. Both shared gluttony: the one from alcoholism, the other from overeating. To Lloyd, in depression, Bill wrote, "The whole success of A.A. has been founded upon suffering; it's not in the least the great American success story."[77] Radically countercultural. Bill in his commentary on Step Eleven, "Sought through prayer..." spoke of suffering as the key to growth.

> Even when we have tried hard and failed, we may chalk that up as one of the greatest credits of all. Under these conditions, the pains of failure are converted into assets. Out of them we receive the stimulation we need to go forward. Someone who knew what he was talking about once remarked that pain was the touchstone of all spiritual progress. How heartily we AA's can agree with him, for we know that the pains of drinking had to come before sobriety, and emotional turmoil before serenity.[78]

That "someone," most probably Father Ed, would see this ballpark as "Glad Gethsemene," where he would bring his suffering to the Cross of Christ. Father Ed in his personal vision of Steps Six and Seven saw suffering this way.

> I think the sixth step is the one which divides the men from the boys in A.A. It is the love of the cross. The sixth step says that one is not almost, but entirely ready; not merely willing, but ready. The difference is between wanting and willing to have God remove all these defects of character. You have here...not the willingness of Simon of Cyrene to suffer, but the great desire or love, similar to what Chesterton calls "Christ's love affair with the cross."

> The seventh step implements that desire by humbly asking God to remove these defects.... And so that continuing detachment which goes along and in any ascetical life, holds true in A.A. As one grows in A.A. the problems seem to be bigger, the strength bigger, and the dividends greater.[79]

Father Ed spoke to what Bill was going through: continuing detachment, pain/growth followed by, on a deeper level, more pain/growth. Father Ed had written Bill in 1942 that progress in the spiritual life was "not through achievement but detachment." Depression — the hard way — taught Bill more detachment and discernment.

In letters Bill wrote to others suffering depression, he frequently suggested the sufferer try everything: vitamin B3, walking and breathing, meditation, the Twelve Steps. Dealing with the fear of depression, he says to Bill H. from Texas, "Easy does it, first things first; do what we can. Believe me, I too have been through the wringer."

Bill began to discern the value of his depression. In a letter to George, Bill said of his depression, "Actually, my sickness kept me off the road and prevented me from turning myself into an AA big shot. The great lesson I learned was that suffering can be highly beneficial to the sufferer and to those about them if only it can be realized that the experiences are a necessary part of development."[80]

To Lisa, suffering from depression, he wrote what he had learned from his own suffering.

> At the time of my depression I thought my only virtue was sobriety, my depression being so deep. Yet the sense of responsibility I had for going on and for holding up my end of the A.A. deal kept me more or less at work. Sometimes I could be quite paralyzed, other times I could get a good deal done....
>
> I say this to you because pain is the touchstone of practically all progress. Now pain is something that can be destructive, if you let it be — but I see you are not doing this — you keep trying. Therefore, you are going

to make something constructive out of it; you are going to have a special mission, perhaps to people who are suffering the kind of isolation you seem to be having. But I am completely confident that if you persist, you will break out of this isolation.

And believe me, I well understand what it is. This much I wanted to let you know.[81]

This constructive special mission in Bill's case did not come without a struggle. He wrote in a 1954 letter, "I used to be ashamed of my condition and so didn't talk about it. But nowadays I freely confess I am a depressive, and this has attracted other depressives to me. Working with them has helped a great deal."[82]

In the 1958 *Grapevine* article, "The New Frontier: Emotional Sobriety," Bill writes:

I asked myself, "Why can't the Twelve Steps work to release me from this unbearable depression?" By the hour, I stared at the St. Francis prayer: "It is better to comfort than to be comforted."

Suddenly, I realized what the answer might be. My basic flaw had always been dependence on people or circumstances to supply me with prestige, security, and confidence. Failing to get these things according to my perfectionistic dreams and specifications, I fought for them. And when defeat came, so did my depression.

Reinforced by what grace I could find in prayer, I had to exert every ounce of will and action to cut off these faulty emotional dependencies upon people and upon circumstances. Then only could I be free to love as Francis had loved.[83]

Sometime about 1953, Bill commented in his letters on how he faced this issue of dependency on others for security, romance, approval. He distilled his complete statement on dependency and depression in his 1958 article, "The New Frontier: Emotional Sobriety." Ernie Kurtz offers three of these letters on the dependency issue in his *Not God: A History of Alcoholics Anonymous.*[84]

Bill wrote one of these letters to Marion on March 31, 1953. "Since I have begun to pray that God may release me from absolute dependence on anybody, anything, or any set of circumstances, I have begun to do so much better that it amounts to a second conversion experience." That April he wrote Jeff:

> I am beginning to see that all my troubles have their root in a habitual and absolute dependence upon my personal prestige, security, and romantic attachment. When these things go wrong, there is depression. Now this absolute dependence upon people and situations for emotional security is, I think, the immense and devastating fallacy that makes us miserable. This craving for such dependencies, this utter dependence upon people and situations, can only lead to conflict. Both on the surface and at depth. We are making demands on circumstances and people that are bound to fail us. The only safe and sure channel of absolute dependence is upon God himself.

Bill came to see that facing his dependency issues meant becoming free from depression. He wrote on April 6, 1953, to Gladys in England:

> The central curative idea was that I didn't have to be dependent, in any absolute sense, upon any particular person, groups of persons, or set of circumstances to be a whole person, a going human concern. I realize that the basic defect of my life had been a craving to depend absolutely upon the instinctual rewards of a place in society, material and emotional security, also, the right romance. Consciously and unconsciously, I had always demanded these things as a condition of happiness. The only absolute that we can depend on is God's love....
>
> Then when I became willing to let go of demands and substitute for them an outgoing love as best I could show it, just as one would in a 12th step case, to that extent I became liberated and to that extent did I re-

ceive the gifts of proper instinctual satisfaction. This is what I have been pondering most of late. And when I realized it and felt the truth of it, and became more willing to practice love in this manner, my brief depression came to an abrupt end. The skies cleared for me as never before.

Suffering led Bill to sobriety and other suffering alcoholics. Further recovery led him to more suffering, his own depression and reaching out to other "depressives." This led to discernment, both for himself and for AA. As Bill said earlier in his letter to Lisa, "Sometimes I could be quite paralyzed [with depression], other times I could get a good deal done. Actually, this was very good for AA. It kept me off the big-time speaking circuit; it made me sit home and wonder what was going to become of me and of the fellowship. This was the beginning of the formation of the AA traditions."

Facing his own recovery issues on deeper levels let Bill begin discarding his false self, his dependencies. Dowling stayed with Bill on this journey to his true self. That is the point Dowling made to Bill in their first meeting: God was doing something special in him. Bill was not to block that movement. Friends support the movement to the true self.[85] On that journey both men learned discernment.

Bill in his letter to Ollie talks of his respect for Karen Horney.

You interest me very much when you talk of Karen Horney. I have the highest admiration of her. That gal's insights have been most helpful to me. Also for the benefit of screwballs like ourselves, it may be that someday we shall devise some common denominator of psychiatry — of course, throwing away their much abused terminology — common denominators which neurotics could use on each other. The idea would be to extend the moral inventory of AA to a deeper level, making it an inventory of psychic damages, reliving in conversation episodes, etc. I suppose someday a Neurotics Anonymous will be formed and will actually do all this.[86]

Later in June of the same year, 1956, he suggested to Ollie that they do an "inventory of psychic damages, actual episodes: inferiority, shame, guilt, anger and relive (them) in our minds to reduce them." Bill added the heading would be from the "bridge of identification" with another.

The assumption: two people with the same wound by telling their stories can heal each other. One image of the healing came in a letter from "Jones" to Bill W. He sends Bill some material on Karen Horney's *Neurosis and Human Growth*.[87] Jones talked in his letter about the glory drive for prestige and the perfect father. Then he talks about using a blueprint to put together a new car. "To give a happy ending to my little allegory, he puts the engine on wheels and drives off in one direction—the one directed by his real self, not pride, sex dependency, compulsive choice, or over-dependency. He puts them together and makes the damn thing run."

This car is running—not in a purple haze—but for daylight. To M.J., Bill had written, "Keep at it, my boy, with the grace of God you can find the light again."[88] To Gladys he wrote, "Then, when I became willing to let go of demands on anybody or upon circumstances and substitute for them an outgoing love as best I could show it, just as one would in a 12 step case, to that extent I became liberated and to that extent did I receive the gifts of proper instinctual satisfaction. This is the line I've been pondering much of late. And when I realized it, and felt the truth of it, and became more willing to practice love in this manner, my brief depression came to an abrupt end, and the skies cleared for me as never before."[89]

CHAPTER 7

Boundaries:
Mr. AA and Bill Wilson

Bill updated Dowling on his own depression. "Little by little I seem to be getting out of the clutches of the Devil — or whatever it was had hold of me the last couple of years. The past few weeks have been the best yet. Though I can visualize the benefits of the suffering involved, I am still unable to say that I got any great joy out of the experience while it was going on." Bill added, "This informs me loudly that I have a hell of a long way before catching up with some of the guys I read about (and see) in that astounding outfit of yours!"

Bill continued in the letter to Father Ed that he looked forward to his coming to New York that summer as part of the annual Summer School of Catholic Action. About the Cana Conference that Dowling founded for families, Bill wrote that he was more and more impressed. "The concept seemed mighty sound and the need crying." Nothing yet had been done on the family level except for some informal gatherings of wives and children while their spouses were at AA meetings.[90]

Bill wrote next on July 31, 1946, to thank Dowling for his suggestions on The Twelve Points of Tradition for AA. Bill had been trying to prepare for when "Smith and I shuffle off this mortal coil" by restructuring power from the co-founders and trustees to the body of AA. Bill asked for Dowling's input and wrote that the trustees were strongly split on the issue. The trustees thought that Bill and Dr. Bob and the trustee board (nonalcoholic members in the majority) would continue as the AA authority. Bill wanted the authority to be more grassroots. Dowling agreed.

Bill and Lois were "starting off tomorrow for two months on a vacation trip by automobile, which will include no AA stops." He was sorry they would miss seeing Dowling in New York. Bill seemed to be taking more vacations, taking more time for his private priorities, and saying "no" to the expectations of others.

Sometime in 1947 Bill began to see a psychiatrist, Frances Weeks. He would see her on Fridays and then on Saturday see Bishop Sheen for instructions about the Catholic faith. Bill had been introduced to Bishop Sheen through Fulton and Grace Oursler. Oursler was the editor of *Liberty* magazine, which ran an early piece on AA, "Alcoholics and God."

To a friend he wrote how Frances Weeks challenged him to clarify his boundaries and leave room for his private self.

> Her thesis is that my position in AA has become quite inconsistent with my needs as an individual. Highly satisfactory to live one's life for others, it cannot be anything but disastrous to live one's life for others as those others think it should be lived. One has, for better or worse, to choose his own life. The extent to which the AA movement and individuals in it determine my choices is really astonishing. Things which are primary to me (even for the good of AA) are unfulfilled. I'm constantly diverted to secondary or even useless activities by AA's whose demands seem to them primary, but are not really so. So we have the person of Mr. Anonymous in conflict with Bill Wilson. To me, this is more than an interesting speculation — it's homely good sense.[91]

Pass It On quotes a page from Lois's diary to indicate how Bill had let himself be overwhelmed by the demands of others and ended up running around putting out the next "forest fire."

> Bill, Helen, and Eb left for town. Bill left saying that if anyone came to him with another problem, he'd scream. Soon after they left, Dot [Bill's sister] phoned saying

she had the most awful letter from her mother, who had been told the March Issue of the *Grapevine* said we were on our way out there (which it does not), that we had not let her know, that she had borrowed $75,000, etc., etc., etc. Dot said she thought she should fly right out, as she was afraid of suicide. Bill pulled ropes and got her a plane reservation for 2:30. She missed the train to N.Y. and Kitty drove her all the way. Everybody was phoning everybody else. I wired Freddy B. about Mother. Dot should arrive in 12 hours. Helen came home, and Zerelda spent the night again. Bill sandwiched in getting Dot on the plane and Sibley out of Bellevue and off to High Watch Farm.[92]

Bill struggled with being overly responsible for others as he tried to separate his private from his public person. He took more time for himself. He took vacations with Lois, usually in Vermont. On another level, the issue was: could he make important choices for himself as an individual, separate from the public "Mr. AA"? The next chapter treats one such issue, his consideration to join the Catholic Church.

Meanwhile, Dowling continued as AA's ambassador, now to the world of journalism. In his newspaper column, Westbrook Pegler, a journalist friend of Dowling's, had referred to the founder of AA as "wet-brained" and his followers as "effectively deluded." Dowling took Pegler on in a letter of July 21, 1947. "I think you hit below the belt. I understand that the founding father had a good laugh over it but some of his pals were taken aback. Not only has he done an awful lot of good but he really is an 18-karat fellow." Dowling did not take those who put down Bill Wilson or AA lightly.

For his part, Bill's friendship and admiration for Father Ed led him to take a serious look at the Catholic Church. Bill sensed in the Catholic Church a security that he resisted but wanted. Bill's struggle with this question (and his boundaries) is next.

CHAPTER 8

Bill and the Catholic Church

That fall (September 3, 1947) Bill wrote he was just back from a two-month vacation between Nantucket and Vermont and "Can't recall a vacation which has left us both so much better." In his letter Bill said he did not see how to get over the "gang plank" and into the Catholic Church, though "I'm affected more than ever by that sweet and powerful aura of the Church, that marvelous spiritual essence flowing down the centuries." The doctrine of papal infallibility stopped him, though he admitted to attributing more to infallibility than was strictly there.

On Saturdays he was taking instruction from Bishop Sheen, whose "deep conviction, great power, and learning" impressed Wilson. "He really practices what he preaches," and Bill "appreciated being with him." At the end of the letter he added a P.S. "Oh, if the Church only had a fellow-traveler department, a cozy spot where one could warm his hands at The Fire and bite off only as much as he could swallow. Maybe I'm just one more shopper looking for a bargain on that virtue — Obedience." Dowling's response merited including his whole letter here.

September 8, 1947

Bill:

Of course there is a fellow-traveler department, even as AA has a fellow-traveler department. Christ's church is not for the just and the good, but rather for sinners. "I came not to save the just." And of course the worst boobs in the world are sinners. Just as AA is not for the sober and the good but rather uses the weak and the bad for work, so Christ has always been associated with the weak, the poor and the human, from his nine months stay in the womb of his mother, to his years with his bungling, ostentatious, little college of twelve cardinals. [We] would go out of business if everyone were sensible and good and unselfish, but it is made up of human clay and it takes a very [little] tolerance to understand its adjectival errors and mistakes.[93]

[When] you die, AA will cling to your substantive spirit and will continue to make the same percentage of irritating — to the non-alcoholic — mistakes. So Christ's Church today will have as one of its marks the presence of sinners and the weak, few and pontiff.

As the non-alcoholic must not be scandalized at the human in and even the sub-human selfishness, so you must not be scandalized at the human in Christ's followers.

The road to truth has never been better charted than Christ charted it. "Live in My way and you will know the truth."

I believe that for you that way is lodemarked by the 12 steps; especially for those who can pray by the 7th step; for the more privileged who cannot pray easily, by the 6th step.

I believe there is a priesthood of husband to wife and wife to husband. The Catholic Church teaches that on their wedding day the minister or priest of the sacrament of matrimony is the couple themselves. As for other priestly functions, Lois is the important key to the solution of your worries these days. Give her my love.

Sincerely,
Edward Dowling, S.J.

Dowling pulled back to a wider frame. He backed off from Bill's broken record on the infallibility issue and emphasized instead a larger God who came for sinners. Both the Catholic Church and AA would have sinful people. The important thing would be to walk in the truth revealed to Bill, namely, God's intervention within the Twelve Steps, and to live out his relationship as husband to Lois. The message is the same as on the first night they met, November 1940, when Dowling called Bill to accept God's personal revelation to him. Dowling deeply respected that revelation and Bill's response. Dowling continually called Bill to surrender to the care behind that call. Dowling was saying, "Leave off the *mind games,* taking the Church's inventory; surrender to the action of God's grace, intervening in you, now."

Bill responded six days later, "Thanks so much for your good letter of Sept. 8. You always catch me where the hair is short. As though I had standing to confess anyone's sins!" He said as an ex-drunk he was not scandalized by the sins of the Church but by "the inability of the Church to confess its own sins." "Did I not think so seriously of joining, I wouldn't even think of raising the question."

It is ever so hard to believe that any human beings, no matter who, are able to be infallible about anything. There seems to be so little evidence all through the centuries that God intends to work that way. Naturally He could if He would. But would He — or did He? I can understand one would find enormous security and assurance if one could affirmatively believe that proposition. But the Church asks those who would embrace her to believe it implicitly. It is the affirmative step in this direction I find so difficult.

Bill added, "There is no one in the world among all my spiritual contacts I would rather share the hours with. If I ever come to the Faith, I am sure it will be through the demonstration of those in it like you." Bill closed with his good news, "There has been a most marvelous change within the last sixty days in me. I feel fully alive again."

Dowling's answer of October 1, 1947, came right to the point: whether or not God can intervene and under what limits infallibility operates.

> You are so right that "it is ever so hard to believe that any human beings are able to be infallible about anything." Infallibility is more than human. It calls for an intervention by a Power greater than ourselves. As I understand it, it does not mean that the teaching body of the Church will talk horse sense but that it is protected from formally teaching moral nonsense.

Then Dowling focused on God's merciful interventions, which Bill and others in AA had experienced.

> Even as you in the hospital witnessed a superhuman intervention for the sake of a relatively unimportant quantity of people, so the point you correctly make that human infallibility, as hopeless, would seem to force a merciful and just Father to intervene. Historically, there have been superhuman interventions — yourself, Horace Crystal, The Incarnation.

Dowling, who in 1955 during his talk at the AA Twentieth Anniversary in St. Louis, traced the steps of God intervening on behalf of humanity through the Incarnation, claimed the Incarnation was like Bill's conversion in Towns Hospital. God's love can intervene *because Bill has experienced this*. Again Dowling shifted to a much larger frame: God loving and intervening, whether by infallibility or by a conversion experience. The focus is no longer infallibility, but God's breaking through with spiritual experiences to humanity.

Dowling added that he saw a "tremendous amount of implicit faith involved in explicit doubt or rejection." He also mentioned that he had been interviewed for a Queen's Work pamphlet on AA by Frank Riley. He hopes "it will bring to the attention of priests the AA availability."

Bill answered on October 14, 1947, that he believed in interventions, but only those "confirmed by experience — the Resurrection and return, the healing miracles, spiritual experiences themselves." He did not believe in what was beyond human experience: the Virgin birth, Christ's blood and body in the Mass, infallibility.

> So, in this case, I have a positive aversion to the idea. I seem congenitally unable to believe that any human beings have the right to claim unqualified authority and infallibility about anything, whether dogma, morals, or politics. I suppose my Yankee ancestry is showing up here with its special egotism and infallibility.

Bill's letter showed his resistance, deeper than reason. Dowling responded on October 4, 1947, in good humor, "You have my shoulders pinned down on that infallibility matter, but it takes two out of three falls to win. I think I will back off and try to get my wind."

> I cannot imagine the doctrine was ever conceived as a bid for popularity, but if it is true it is "precious" and should be announced. In one of the few formal uses of it that I can recall at the present the Papacy enunciated a most difficult doctrine, that some — many — find uselessly irritating, when it proclaimed the doctrine of the Immaculate Conception, the exemption of Christ's mother from the taint of original sin. It was years later at Lourdes that the apparition of Mary announced, "I am the Immaculate Conception," and then as now at Lourdes the blind see and the lame walk.
>
> The road to truth is probably through the eye of a needle, calling for deflation until littleness. I wonder if both our steps now and all successful next steps could not be as humiliating as the acceptances we balk at.

Dowling reminded them both: the way to grace is the same; acceptance of deflation and littleness — the eye of the needle and God's love. This time Dowling again reframed the question in the larger yet down-home experience: humanity needs humility to experience God's action. Bill needed deflation before his Towns spiritual experience of God's love.

In his next letter, November 5, 1947, Bill expressed concern about Dowling's health and ordered fifty of the new Queen's Work AA pamphlets. Dowling responded on November 26 with typical humor about his health. "I feel fine. When people say I look bum, it is usually because I need a shave." Then he picked up on Bill's distinction between his head and heart.

> As you say, you feel like a Catholic. This I know. But I doubt if you think like a Protestant. If you did, you would be at Sunday services at a Protestant church and subscribing to that code and creed. Protestant with a capital P is not only negative but also positive. I think you may be a protestant, spelled with a small p, which is happy, but semi.[94]

Bill's next letter to Dowling of April 8, 1948, included a long letter to Clem Lane, Dowlings's Catholic Chicago newspaper friend, concerning Bill's feelings about the Catholic Church. "Bishop Sheen has always insisted that people come to the Church on the basis of reason. I do not see how that could happen in my case. There seem to be several potent reasons for not doing so. Only an overwhelming interior sense of the rightness of such a course could move me."

There had and has always been this tension in the Catholic Church about faith. Some saw faith as a movement of the intelligence by word or signs to permit access to unseen realities. Others saw faith as a confidence directed to a faithful person involving the whole person.[95] Somehow Bill had gotten to spinning reasons around the infallibility pole and could not pull out to a larger picture.

Bill, at the end of his letter to Clem Lane, stated clearly his own mission. "I believe that my duty would lie in helping the non-Catholic alcoholic to discover the grace of God."[96] Dowling's answering letter of April 15, 1948, confirmed Bill in that calling. "I have a feeling that anyone who sincerely tries to apply the 12 steps is following in Christ's footsteps with the result which Christ promised when he said, 'Dwell in My way and you will know the truth.'"

Dowling added, "the addiction to money and the addiction to power is one and the same thing." Dowling noted, "St. Ignatius in his Two Standards meditation says the same thing."[97] Then he called Bill to surrender to God's care for the whole of the AA movement.

> Bill, I do not think you seem to be as second and third step on headquarters as you are on alcoholism. Could it be that the "Power" of the second step and the God of the third, fifth, sixth, seventh and eleventh steps is not powerful enough to handle headquarters: I know this has been a worry to you.

Bill included in his next letter a mimeographed sheet to AA friends dated January 20, 1949. It was a plea from "Dr. Bob and me that when we have finished the few special assignments still left us, we thenceforth be regarded as simple AA's and not at all as founders." Bill had been trying to regain his health and knew that he had to cut back on speaking, group visiting, and extensive correspondence. Dowling wrote back and forth to Bobbie Berger, Bill's secretary at the AA office, and found that Bill was seeing Dr. Bob in Akron about an old cause: how to pass the AA power to the group or a service conference and not just the trustees and the co-founders.

This section of letters added something new. Dowling makes it clear: Bill's call is to be faithful to the God calling him to the Twelve Steps. This call was bigger than organized religion. Dowling would have Bill follow that special Twelve-Step calling. Furthermore, Dowling has reframed Bill's question on infallibility. Dowling claimed they were wrestling in their arguments about religion. Bill had won two out of three falls. Then Dowling turned the tables. Wilson had been arguing over the little part of the wrestling mat called "Catholic." Dowling showed him the whole mat, where a loving God had called Bill to follow his own Twelve Steps as a way of walking in His truth and bringing AA to the world.

The whole mat was graced — not just the Catholic section. Bill could fall anywhere, wrestle with his God, and receive Grace for the world. Bill will say later, "It is characteristic of him (Dowling) that he has never, in all these years, asked me to join his church."[98] Bill was off the Catholic hook yet on the God hook where God called him and AA—without trusting money or power—to move forward. On this big mat, falls anywhere lead to grace everywhere because God's Son stepped down to a mat called "planet earth." A Merry Christmas, indeed.

CHAPTER 9

The Spiritual Exercises and the Traditions

As a help for his work on the *Twelve Steps and Twelve Traditions,* Bill asked Dowling for a copy of *The Spiritual Exercises of St. Ignatius.*[99] Dowling, in the hospital for a retinal stroke, could not read. His sister, Anna, read him the manuscript drafts Bill sent. Dowling wanted to get well for a trip to Ireland that fall.

In his next letter Dowling thanked Bill for Christmas thoughtfulness and prayed, "May 1952 bring us closer together by bringing us closer to the power of the second step, the God of the third, fifth, sixth, seventh steps, the Christ of Christmas." It was a good way to start the year: pledging to trust the power of God in the Steps. In closing Dowling mentioned he would be giving a retreat for AA women at the New York Cenacle and hoped then to visit Bill and Lois.[100]

On May 20, 1952, Bill wrote to Dowling with a draft copy of twelve essays on the traditions.

> A group of similar essays, covering the twelve steps. A few people think that the Traditions aren't covered with enough dignity — that posterity may not like them for that reason. However, we feel that we are writing for the information of alcoholics who ordinarily have no time to read anything much except as it concerns their own survival. Our idea is to publish the Twelve Steps and these Twelve Traditions in a small book to appear,

I hope, by next fall. If we are able to do a fair job on the Steps, that will be helpful and, published along with the Traditions, they may act as a bait for reading the latter. However, we'll see.

Bill added, "We'd very much like your criticisms of the material enclosed. Do we run across the grain of your ideas anywhere, do you care for the writing style and is the structural situation depicted in conformity with your observation of AA?" Bill mentioned he had good help from some other writers, Tom Powers, Betty Love, and Jack Alexander. He wanted Dowling's input, "no punches pulled," and ended the letter with a request for *The Spiritual Exercises of St. Ignatius.*

Have done two of the Twelve Steps. Considering I am such a shabby practitioner of them, it is strange they seem to be going better than the Traditions. But in this connection, we'd like to give the Ignatian Exercises some real study. What books or pamphlets would you suggest in that connection? On the Steps, I know of no one who might help as you can. Will you lend us a hand?

Dowling answered on May 27, 1952, "Complimented at being asked to comment on the Traditions manuscript." He did not know of "any reading book on the Spiritual Exercises — none but the dry text. The best text with an official commentary is *The Spiritual Exercises of St. Ignatius* edited by the Episcopalian clergyman, W. H. Longridge."[101]

Then Dowling commented on the Tradition One essay.[102] "I like its brevity, sanity. The Rickenbacker life boat paragraph might make a better first paragraph." In the Tradition One commentary Bill told the story of Captain Eddie Rickenbacker's plane crashing in the Pacific. Members of the crew found themselves saved from death and floating in a raft on a perilous sea.

They knew their common welfare came first. "None might become selfish of water or bread. Each needed to consider the others, and in their abiding faith they knew they must find their real strength. And this they did find, in measure to transcend all the defects of their frail craft, every test of uncertainty, pain, fear, and despair, and even the death of one."[103]

In the final version Bill placed this paragraph — aware of its punch — second last.

Bill wrote back on June 17, 1952, about how good he felt that Dowling would look over these Traditions. Bill added he was doing 2000-word essays on each of the Twelve Steps and would send these drafts for Dowling to note "major blunders" and "face-lifting suggestions." Bill concluded with a consoling paragraph about AA's Second General Service Conference.

> Things are going real good. That last General Service Conference was a beautiful thing to see. I wish you could have been there. I know you would have shared my confidence that AA can now attend to its central affairs. Since the Conference, I feel unusually secure and happy. It brought a peace of mind such as I have never known since the original experience. I could almost draw a definition of serenity that would stick — even with you!

The conference was Bill's dream to make the Central Office report to elected members of the General AA Fellowship. (In Dowling's words, "Leadership should be on tap, not on top.") He and Dr. Bob could pass on their authority to the Fellowship and step down to become "fellow members." It also meant AA would last once the co-founders in Bill's words, "shuffled off this mortal coil." Bill made this point most clearly at the 1955 International AA Conference in St. Louis. Dowling again and again challenged Bill to trust God's care (Steps 2 and 3) for the whole of AA. Bill was trusting more on God's care in the structure for AA.

In Dowling's next letter on June 20, 1952, he affirmed Bill's consolation, "So glad to hear about the serenity." Dowling added he had been in the hospital for nearly a week with a retinal stroke that made it hard to read. Friends had taped the draft of the traditions so he could critique them. Dowling added, "So glad you are going to do an interpretation of each of the 12 steps."

"I am sending to you today with my compliments *The Spiritual Exercises of St. Ignatius,* Longridge's version." He said he hoped to see Bill when he would be at Fordham University in New York before sailing for England and Ireland on August 21.

Bill wrote on July 17, 1952, that he and Lois were just getting back from a vacation and were concerned about Dowling's hospitalization. Then Bill thanked him for the book on the Exercises.

> Please have my immense thanks for that wonderful volume on the Ignatian Exercises. I'm already well into it, and what an adventure it is! Excepting for a sketchy outline you folks had posted on the Sodality wall years back, I had never seen anything of the Exercises at all. Consequently I am astonished and not a little awed by what comes into sight. Again, thanks a lot.

On a trip to see Father Ed in St. Louis in the early 1940s, Bill went to the Queen's Work office where Dowling had posted on a wall an outline of similarities between the Twelve Steps and The Ignatian Exercises. John Markoe, himself an alcoholic and a Jesuit, had done the outline.[104]

Bill enclosed a draft of the first four Steps for Dowling to look at when his eyes were better. He remarked,

> The problem of the Steps seems a considerable one. The idea has been to broaden and deepen them, both for the newcomers and old-timers. But the angles are so many, it's hard to shoot them rightly. We have to deal with atheists, agnostics, believers, depressives, paranoids, clergymen, psychiatrists, and all and sundry. How to widen the opening so it seems right and reasonable to enter there and at the same time avoid distractions, distortions, and the certain prejudices of all who may read seems fairly much of an assignment.

Bill used this same image of widening the entrance when he talked about Step Two and finding a Higher Power. "The hoop you have to jump through is a lot wider than you think."[105]

In his very next line Bill adds, "But I have good help—of that I am certain. Both over here and over there." The "over there" refers to the spirit world. Bill slipped in this voice from the other world like this was an everyday happening. It was, he said, the voice of Boniface, an apostle from England to Germany, Bavaria, and France, who reformed old church structures, and as bishop with powers from Rome, set up new monasteries and bishoprics. Amazing, that Bill with hangups on the hierarchical church was open to receiving help from a dead bishop.

> One turned up the other day calling himself Boniface. Said he was a Benedictine missionary and English. Had been a man of learning, knew missionary work and a lot about structures. I think he said this all the more modestly but that was the gist of it. I'd never heard of this gentleman but he checked out pretty well in the Encyclopedia. If this one is who he says he is—and of course there is no certain way of knowing—would this be licit contact in your book?

He checked with Dowling to discern the spirit. Bill ended this letter by saying that he is "coming back to earth" (from Boniface) and that Harper was interested in publishing the book.[106] He said he would like to have the "kind of penetration" Dowling could give on the Steps and felt he was doing a job which "if faulty, may never be redone." He added that he hoped Dowling's health would allow him to be in New York on his way to Dublin.

Dowling wrote Bill on July 24, 1952:

> My retinal stroke, sans pain and sans labor, is giving me an enjoyable loaf. I have a reader who comes in so I hope to have the Steps read. I keep feeling that the Steps blueprint the road map of vertical growth of the individual AA.
>
> Boniface sounds like the Apostle of Germany. I still feel, like Macbeth, that these folks tell us truth in small matters in order to fool us in larger. I suppose that is my lazy orthodoxy.

On page 100 of the Longridge edition of the Ignatian Exercises you have the Two Standards Meditation in italics. This meditation caused Leo XIII to assign a prayer at the end of the Mass against the snares of the Devil.

My sister, Anna, is going to be my eyes in England and Ireland — to take dictation, etc.

In a mini-crossword Dowling made he added, "Love to Lois" and asked for AA meeting times and places in England and Ireland.

Dowling always used humor about his health, letting the spotlight be on the needs of the other, not his own. In spite of his bad eyesight he gave Bill some suggestions on the Steps. His acceptance of his own health limits might have said more than any written comments on the Steps.

Dowling saw the *vertical dimension* of AA as working the Steps; he would be the first to claim the *horizontal dimension:* the application of the Twelve Steps to all other compulsions.[107]

Dowling cautioned Bill about the Boniface voice and by his Macbeth quote, asked Bill to watch to what end the voice might lead. The otherworld voices in *Macbeth* tempt Macbeth to power and the murder of the king, Duncan. In the Spiritual Exercises, a person was to watch the beginning, middle, and end of a movement to discern whether the movement was from an evil or a good spirit.[108] Macbeth needed a Dowling!

Lastly, Dowling pointed to one special context in the Exercises, the meditation on the Two Standards, on page 100 in the Longridge version. Ignatius sees the Devil on a high throne surrounded by chaos and smoke, calling all under his flag and control. His way will be to lead them to riches, pride, then to all other vices. Christ, on a low plain, invites all under His flag: to humiliations, poverty, and then to all other blessings.[109] This scene was behind the words Dowling wrote of AA for the dustjacket of the Big Book. "God resists the proud, assists the humble. The shortest cut to humility is humiliations, which AA has in abundance."

In Bill's next letter of August 8, 1952, he mentioned, "I've carefully looked over page 100 of the Longridge you suggested." Bill saw the need for caution in speaking with spirits from the otherworld, agreed in general with the general situation Ignatius presented, but did not want the Church to limit his conversations with the otherworld.

> It doesn't seem reasonable to think that the Devil's agents have such direct and wide open access to us when other well-disposed discarnates including the Saints themselves cannot get through. That is, in any direct way. Since prudent discrimination and good morality is necessary when we deal with people in the flesh, why shouldn't these be the rule with discarnate, too. So motivated, I don't see why the aperture should be so large in the direction of the Devil and so small in the direction of all the good folks who have gone ahead of us. One can't blame the Church for being cautious but I do sometimes wonder if the view isn't rather narrow and even monopolistic. To assume that all communications, not received under Church auspices, are necessarily malign seems going pretty far. I'm not sure the Church says this but that is what the inference always seems to be. I do say this, though, more in the nature of speculation than argument, for the spook business is no longer any burning issue so far as I am concerned. Without inviting it, I still sometimes get an intrusion such as the one I described in the case of the purported Boniface.

Bill held his own with Church authority and with Father Ed, a responsible stance. In 1954, he would decline an honorary doctorate from Yale, in words that indicated he knew the danger of power, honor, riches. "My own life story gathered for years around an implacable pursuit of money, fame, and power, anticlimaxed by my near sinking in a sea of alcohol. Though I survived that grim misadventure, I well understand that the dread neurotic germ of the power contagion has survived in me also."[110] These words are very close to Ignatius in the Meditation on the Two Standards.[111]

In an earlier part of the letter Bill was particularly anxious to get Dowling's view concerning the treatment of Steps Six and Seven.

The problem seemed to be that of persuading folks to make the absolute their objective without losing sight of the fact that most of us will always have to move in the relative. The most we could ask was that all AA's try to discard open rebellion of the "No, Never" variety. That would be to discharge one good pot shot at the absolute while at the same time we reminded ourselves that practically everybody has his sticking point someplace along the line. My observation is that people can get by with a certain amount of postponement but not with outright rebellion. These steps separate the "men from the boys" all right but if a "man" is to be defined as one who is perfectly and continuously willing, then the number of them must be quite small. I'm inclined to define the "man" as the one who has arrived at the point where he can try to be willing in all respects without being whiplashed into it by dire necessity. What we have said in Six and Seven appears to square up with spiritual progress as we see it in AA. But whether we are on all fours with A-1 theology I'm not positive. We really need some advice on this. Maybe you can spare a few moments, when in New York, to check over these two. It would be wonderful if you could.

In Dowling's next letter to Bill (August 9, 1952), he wrote that he had been listening to the Twelve Step essays. "The 12 steps will do a great deal of good. I find them very readable. I do hope the Harper's opportunity develops." Dowling raised a small point, "One question that comes to my mind is so petty. The use of the word 'science' as though inductive, experimental, observational, *a posteriori* science were complete science. But this is microscopic." Bill in his letters on the Catholic Church was so clear in rejecting anything he could not experience inductively. Dowling gently asked him to keep his mind open to another possible way of knowing beyond inductive experience. Dowling concluded:

Please do not construe my brevity as an indication of lack of enthusiasm for the 4 steps which I have played back. My sister, Anna, is going to Europe with me to do my reading, etc. We will be at the Lexington Hotel August 20th and the morning of 21. We sail in the afternoon of August 21 on the America.

Wilson added a handwritten note to this letter asking his secretary to phone this message, "Thanks much your comments on steps. How about lunch or dinner Wednesday, the 20th, with Lois and me at Hotel Lexington. Realize your time short so don't hesitate to turn us down." On this same letter, Bill wrote in his big scrawl, "Saw Ed. He liked steps six and seven."

CHAPTER 10

A Christmas Gift:
The Prayer of St. Francis

Bill's final work on the *Twelve Steps and Twelve Traditions,* Father Ed's talk at the Clergy Conference, and his work with both Cana and Recovery Inc. are the themes for the next dozen letters. Christmas greetings bookend this group of letters. One letter of Bill's — with its distinct "confessional" tone — stands apart.[112]

In his Christmas letter (December 29, 1952) Father Ed addressed both Bill and Lois.

> At this season of the year it is so easy to think back to that New Year's Eve and Day that we had together. The intervening years have cemented our friendship.
>
> I know how much of yourself is in the prayer of Francis of Assisi. This makes your gift more valuable and more deeply appreciated than the beauty of the gift would deserve.
>
> May 1953 bring you and Lois and me closer to God that we may enjoy even greater closeness to each other.

Dowling, with St. Francis, believed his love of Bill and Lois was bound up with the love of God become man at Christmas. As a result any human gesture was of God's love,[113] including memories of their friendship and that special New Year's Day of 1941 when Father Ed was at their home just a month after their first meeting.[114]

Bill gave Father Ed a framed copy of the Prayer of St. Francis, "Lord make me an instrument of Thy Peace."[115] That prayer hung near the window to the left of Bill's desk at Wit's End, his studio. In his essay on Step 11, Bill wrote of a way to pray with a pause after each phrase of "Make me an Instrument of Thy Peace." He may have seen this same method of prayer in the Longridge edition of the Spiritual Exercises which Dowling sent him in 1952.[116] This book was one of about thirty books on a shelf above the window to the left of his studio desk. The bulk of his books were at their Stepping Stones home about fifty feet away from his studio.

This Eleventh Step commentary Bill found hard to write since he was still suffering from depression and could finish only half a page at a session. The prayer of St. Francis, "Lord, Make me a channel of Thy peace," opened up his commentary and framed the service of Step Twelve. The prayer's challenge to service helped relieve his depression.

This service prayed in the prayer of St. Francis was focused sharply in the book next to the Spiritual Exercises on Bill's window shelf: Reuel Howe's *Man's Need and God's Action*.

> It is the new relationship that conveys the power of God in Christ for salvation — a relationship of the redeemed and the redeeming; of the forgiven and the forgiving; of those who freely give out of what they have freely received; of those who having surrendered themselves, have become the instruments of His saving love; of those who, though broken and sinful, are used by Him to heal and save.[117]

At Bill's request Father Ed wrote a letter to the editor of *Harpers* affirming that Catholics would find this new book on the steps and traditions as helpful as the first book, *Alcoholics Anonymous*.[118] To Bill he wrote:

> I suspect that The Steps will be a book to be meditated rather than read. It contains the basic message. The audience identification is there. It has dignity, reverence, and stylistic readability. It has a little bit of the elder statesman smell of the lamp.[119] I sense that it makes a Scylla and Charybdis route between admiring laity in

the boxes and the needy drunks in the gutter. What the religious folk will find in it I do not know. I do not see any headaches along that line. I shall try to compensate with my prayers for my tardiness and inadequacy.

I have been asked to talk at the Clergy Conference on Alcoholism at the retreat house at Jamaica, Long Island, April 8. I hope this trip may give me a chance to see you. I intend to quote from the new manuscript.

In 1949 four priests, Fathers Ralph Pfau, John Dillon, Raymond Atkins, and John Ford, S.J., began the first National Clergy Conference on Alcoholism. The talks and minutes of the conference were published each year in *The Blue Book*. Father Ed had been invited as a speaker, but until April of 1953 the schedule of the Summer School of Catholic Action kept him from attending.

In his next letter Bill wrote a telling paragraph about some other members of the Catholic clergy and what he saw might be the conference atmosphere.

About that Clergy Conference. Because you will be there, I would especially like to go. But I'm really dubious about it. I know that within the Church there are several sharply different viewpoints on what to do about alcohol and the Priest. As I haven't any worthwhile ideas myself, I am a bit reluctant to get in the middle of this specialized subject. When the Clergy Conferences first started I agreed to attend the first but backed off after being severely catechized by the Clergy representative from the New York area respecting my views on free will, Buchmanism, and whether non-alcoholics could fix drunks — etc. In order to get on with the writing I have been declining all speaking invitations and special visits of late.[120]

Dowling chose to walk into this clerical world with its own kind of Scylla and Charybdis: self-righteousness and denial.[121]

Father Ed did give his talk at the April 8, 1953, session.[122] To enter the clerical world, Father Ed played his theological card:

comparing the Twelve Steps to *The Spiritual Exercises of St. Ignatius* and tracing the movement from disordered attachments to freedom, union with God and others. The moving part of the talk was not so much the theology but several telling comments Father Ed made along the way.

Father Ed underlined what he had said on the jacket of the Big Book. "I am sensible, as you are, of God's closeness to human humility. I am sensible, also, of how close human humility can come to humiliation, and I know how close humiliation can come to an alcoholic." Father Ed grounds the movement of the Ignatian Two Standards Meditation that he had shared with Bill: "Humiliations lead to humility and thence to all other blessings." Later, in the same talk he drew on his own experience:

> Alcoholics Anonymous has helped me as a person and as a priest. AA has made my optimism greater. My hopelessness starts much later. Like anyone who has watched AA achieve its goals, I have seen dreams walk. I expect them to walk. You and I know that in the depths of humiliation we are in a natural area, and rightly handled, especially in the inner spirit of that Sixth Step, I think we can almost expect the automatic fulfillment of God's promise to assist the humble. Where there is good will, there is almost an iron connection between humiliation-humility-God's help.[123]

Then Father Ed told of the AA men in St. Louis who challenged him to use the steps to stop his own smoking. He added, if he could "postpone thinking about smoking for three minutes, he would not smoke. One minute at a time."

> That is a humiliating admission for a priest who tells others to give up much harder things. From AA I learned to respect the little suffering of denying the thought of a smoke and to pool that suffering with the sufferings of Christ, in the spirit of the Sixth Step. At that moment, like a breath of fresh air, came the thought of the widow and her mite and the importance which love can give to

unimportant things. With humiliations came humility, and with humility came God's promised help.[124]

Father Ed started like Bill on the Sixth Step. It is "the one which divides the men from the boys." But Father Ed adds his "own take" on this Step (and his own suffering). "It is the love of the Cross," he added, "you have here, if you look into it, not the willingness of Simon Cyrene to suffer, but the great desire or love, similar to what Chesterton calls, 'Christ's love affair with the cross.'"[125]

Brother Malone, a Jesuit brother sacristan at the St. Louis College Church, noted that after Father Ed celebrated his daily Eucharist, he would sit in the sacristy and gaze at a crucifix. Then he got up, went to the nearest phone, and made his appointments for the day. Dowling, like Chesterton, was another big man with a love affair for the cross. In this same talk Father Ed would add his unique window on the steps, "Christ and His Passion came in encouragingly in the Third and Eleventh Steps."[126]

Father Ed treated the question of priest membership in AA with his special twist.

> Frankly, I don't think the Church needs saving nearly as much as this man. God's cause is often hurt by people who are trying to save God. The scandal that a drinking priest might give is not so serious in AA as it would be at a Catholic organization meeting, because the understanding is different."[127]

Dowling is blunt about the gift and wound of the alcoholic priest.

> Priests of AA have two indelible marks: once an alcoholic, always an alcoholic; once a priest, always a priest. Two invisible, indelible marks, both of tremendous significance to others. As alcoholics they know insanity from the inside. As members of AA they know the techniques and they know the wonders that can come from amateur group psychotherapy based on the human will aided by God's help.[128]

Dowling quoted a doctor, "The trouble with you priests is, you all have 'digno-sclerosis,' hardening of the dignity. If you weren't afraid to make a mistake, you'd be out curing people of these things."[129] In the questions and answers after Father Ed's talk, most of the priests fled to the high ground of moralizing: what kind of sin and responsibility was involved in the abuse of alcohol. Dowling stayed on the low ground with his witness to the AA steps for stopping smoking *in his own life.* He called them to walk from head to heart in the valley of humiliations where all blessings flow. As in his dealings with Bill, Father Ed had a touch of Hermes, the divine messenger who helps others through irony and humor to the next truth.[130]

Some time in April of 1953 the two met at America House in New York, the home and workplace of Jesuits who staff *America* magazine. Bill and Father Ed shared a Mass, breakfast and talk. Bill handwrote a note to thank Father Ed:

> After Mass, at breakfast, I saw your face beaded with sweat; due, if I may guess, to physical pain. I then thought that I ought not press my own woes and de-merits upon you. But with characteristic inconsistency, I turned about and did just that. Forthwith, I received the demonstration so characteristic of you: that however you may dislike the sin (about which you said nothing) you surely make the sinner feel understood and loved as no other mortal in my life can. What a Grace![131]

Possibly the "sin" Bill speaks of might be his overdependence on women. This would fit the "confessional" tone of the letter.

If this is true, the letter showed Bill struggling with other compulsions. Father Ed, for his part, respected the confidentiality of whatever Bill revealed at that meeting. In his answering letter Father Ed made these noncommittal remarks:

> Your coming to America House, 329 W. 108, New York and permitting me to share some of your deepest thoughts was a very much appreciated privilege.
> The impression my pretzel-like arthritis gives of being painful brings good dividends in attention, and I

am just enough of a fakir to enjoy it. The truth is that I have the stiffest and most painless arthritis in history. It is an ideal combination.

Had a very hasty in and out of New York last week for a Cana retreat from Friday to Sunday for seven couples. Sometime we might attempt it with a half dozen or more AA couples.

I shall be in New York at our Summer School of Catholic Action August 17 to 22. Would love to see you and Lois.[132]

That sharing (of "sin" in Bill's words) shows the worst can be received not in judgment but acceptance and confidentiality. Behind all this was Bill's dependency relationships with women. He had spoken of this dependency in writing about both his first girlfriend, Bertha and his wife, Lois.[133] In 1958 he spoke of his own dependence on approval and romance as something he needed to face.[134] In his essay on Step Twelve Bill talked about the alcoholic husband's relationship to his wife in words that may have described his own with Lois.

If the man is affected, the wife must become the head of the house, often the breadwinner. As matters get worse, the husband becomes a sick and irresponsible child who needs to be looked after and extricated from endless scrapes and impasses. Very gradually, and usually without any realization of the fact, the wife is forced to become the mother of an erring boy. And if she had a strong maternal instinct to begin with, the situation is aggravated. Obviously not much partnership can exist under these conditions. The wife usually goes on doing the best she knows how, but meanwhile the alcoholic alternately loves and hates her maternal care.[135]

Bill saw the salvation for the couple in working the Steps, the one in AA, the other in Al-Anon. Bill discussed his dependency issue in several letters written the same year as his "confessional" letter.[136]

I know that my underlying difficulty from which all others stem and are merely symptomatic, is that inner insistence which demands that I either be absolutely dependent upon someone, or else dominate them. The latter being merely the reverse side of the coin whose main face is "absolute dependence." Since I have begun to pray that God may release me from absolute dependence on anybody, anything, or any set of circumstances, I have begun to do so much better that it amounts to a second conversion experience.[137]

I am beginning to see that all my troubles have their root in a habitual and absolute dependence upon my personal prestige, security, and romantic attachment. When these things go wrong, there is depression. Now this absolute dependence upon people and situations for emotional security is, I think, the immense and devastating fallacy that makes us miserable. This craving for such dependencies, this utter dependence upon people and situations, can only lead to conflict. Both on the surface and at depth. We are making demands on circumstances and people that are bound to fail us. The only safe and sure channel of absolute dependence is upon God himself.[138]

Bill, facing his own dependency issues, offered hope for others working this same dependency issue in recovery. By facing this issue, he was living at a deeper level the dynamic in the meditation on the Two Standards. The "riches" that can lead a person to pride and all other evils are dependence on others for approval and romance. Bill was grounded where all blessings flow, humility.

Father Ed in his next letter referred to a big blessing: Bill's book was out. He had just received three copies of the *Twelve Steps and Twelve Traditions*. He thanked Bill for the kind dedication and for the extra copies. One copy, he promised, will go to Rattigan's Pub, Kilroosy, Ballag, Roscommon, Ireland. He told of this pub in a *Grapevine* article. Dowling met an Irish mother in the back room of Rattigan's Pub. She had received an AA book and a letter from an American AA reassuring her that her emigrant son had found sobriety in America.[139] Therefore, one copy to Rattigan's. Dowling does not mention Kilroosy was the seat of his Dowling ancestors.

The summer letters from Bill amounted to Bill asking to use a quotation from Father Ed's 1947 pamphlet on AA after the foreword of the second edition of the Big Book. Father Ed was flattered and gave permission to use this paragraph.

> Alcoholics Anonymous is natural; it is natural at the point where nature comes closest to the supernatural, namely in humiliations and in consequent humility. There is something spiritual about an art museum or a symphony, and the Catholic Church approves of our use of them. There is something spiritual about AA too. Catholic participation in it almost invariably results in poor Catholics becoming better Catholics.[140]

This section ended with Father Ed's 1953 Christmas letter to Bill and Lois. This had been a fruitful year: the *Twelve Steps and Twelve Traditions* was born. Dowling himself was moving well in St. Louis as midwife for groups. He wrote of these groups:

> Had a fine evening at the AA Club on the 17th, the Christmas meeting. Planning to spend New Year's Eve there too.
> The Recovery Inc. people borrow strength from the 12 Steps. They, like AA, find that an awful lot of their success is built around home situations.
> Last month we experimented with a Cana Conference, confined to couples from AA, Recovery Inc., Divorcees Anonymous, and Cana.
> They discussed in small groups, three or four couples each and then processed to new groupings. The case presented involved money, in-laws, jealousy, sex. Then asked the question, "What could AA contribute to this situation?" What would Recovery? What would Cana? What would Divorcees Anonymous?
> For our similar Cana Conference on January 3 we shall probably use the January issue of the *Ladies Home Journal* which Popenoe puts out. I thought Lois might be interested for the Al-Anon grouping.

I wish I could spend another New Year's day with you as I did a few years ago.

Father Ed's new life in groups, Bill's in a book. Not a bad way to celebrate: democracy, birthing, wounded healers; a Merry Christmas.

CHAPTER 11

Is This God Speaking?

Without ever knowing the word, many in AA practice discernment. They prefer to talk about "keeping on the path" or keeping "on the beam." Even without the "correct" words they find themselves part of an age-old tradition of discerning people. These people have an inner awareness of centered or not-centered energy. This awareness comes from an accumulated awareness of who they really are. They know where their center is and where it is not, their true self and false self. They know how to flow with their life center.[141] A Quaker group uses these words to speak of this tradition.

> *Discernment* comes from the Latin word *discernere,* which means "to separate," "to distinguish," "to determine," "to sort out." In classical spirituality, discernment means identifying what spirit is at work in a situation; The Spirit of God or some other spirit. Discernment is "sifting through" our interior and exterior experiences to determine their origin. Discernment helps a person understand the source of a call, to whom it is directed, its content, and what response is appropriate. Discernment also involves learning if one is dodging a call, is deaf to a call, or is rejecting a call.[142]

Many of the Dowling/Wilson letters dealt with discernment issues: Bill's dilemma on whether or not to enter the army (chap.

4), how to take time from AA for himself, (chap. 7), can God intervene in a person's life (chap. 8), how to deal with spirits from the otherworld (chap. 4, chap. 9). Dowling is clear about his framework for discernment: greater and greater detachment (chap. 4), and the way of humility from the Two Standards meditation of Ignatius (chap. 10).

The steps of AA presuppose a God whose plans can be known. Step Three says, "made a decision to turn our will and our lives over to the care of God." Step Eleven again underlines that God's will *exists* and that we can *know* it through prayer. "Sought through prayer and meditation to improve our conscious contact with God as we understood Him, praying only for knowledge of *His will for us* and the power to carry that out." (Italics mine.) The presupposition of these steps is a caring God whose will can be known. The big question is: how do I know God is speaking, revealing Himself now in these feelings, desires, in this particular decision.[143]

The daily inventory, Step Ten, asks us to give thanks for our day, check (discern) the interior movements, and in particular mentions spot checks for resentments, "big shotism," and fear. These negative movements are to be balanced by noting "things well done."[144] Ignatius in his Spiritual Exercises had this same exercise now referred to as "The Consciousness Examen."[145] This exercise helps a person to be aware of the movements or promptings in one's day and to pray for help in changing any destructive patterns. Father Ed as a Jesuit would have made this examen twice a day.[146]

Bill had already faced this question in naming his own experience in Towns Hospital as of God. He had prayed for God's help. Light and peace, the same peace experienced at Winchester Cathedral, flooded the hospital room. Then through reading William James's *The Varieties of Religious Experience* and through talking with Dr. Silkworth, he was convinced this experience was *of God*. He learned two key principles: the need to open spiritual experience to others, and that peace/serenity helped confirm the experience to be *of God*.[147]

Not only could God reveal His will to an individual, Bill learned, but God could speak in and through the group. This important discernment came to Bill before he met Father Ed. Bill wrote in Tradition Two, "For our group purpose there is but one ultimate authority — a loving God as He may express Himself in our group conscience. Our leaders are but trusted servants; they do not govern." In his commentary on this tradition, Bill told the story of his job offer from Charlie Towns (hospital director) to be a paid alcoholism counselor for Towns Hospital. Bill asked Charlie for some time to consider the offer. As Bill was racing back home on the subway, he experienced what seemed to be divine guidance: a voice in his head kept saying a sentence right out of the Bible, "The laborer is worthy of his hire." Bill told the story this way...

It was meeting night.... At once I burst into the story of my opportunity. Never shall I forget their impassive faces, and the steady gaze they focused upon me. With waning enthusiasm, my tale trailed off to the end. There was a long silence.

Almost timidly, one of my friends began to speak. "We know how hard up you are, Bill. It bothers us a lot. We've often wondered what we might do about it. But I think I speak for everyone here when I say that what you now propose bothers us an awful lot more.... Don't you realize," he went on, "that you can never become a professional? As generous as Charlie has been to us, don't you see that we can't tie this thing up with his hospital or any other? You tell us that Charlie's proposal is ethical. Sure, it's ethical, but what we've got won't run on ethics only; it has to be better. Sure, Charlie's idea is good but it isn't good enough. This is a matter of life and death, Bill, and nothing but the very best will do!" Challengingly, my friends looked at me as their spokesman continued, "Bill, haven't you often said right here in this meeting that sometimes the good is the enemy of the best? Well, this is a plain case of it. You can't do this thing to us!"

Bill concluded that the Spirit had spoken in the group conscience. He added "the voice on the subway was not *the voice of God.* Here was the true voice, welling up out of my friends. I listened, and — thank God — I obeyed."[148]

In *Alcoholics Anonymous Comes of Age* Bill told of a one-on-one discernment with Father Ed. Bill had been struggling since the publication of the Big Book to decide whether or not to claim his one-third stock interest and have his royalty from the book. He went back and forth on the issue and finally put the case to Father Ed when he turned up in New York.

> Dowling asked, "Do you think AA requires your full-time efforts?" I replied, "Yes, I think it does perhaps indefinitely." Then he inquired, "Could you become a paid therapist, taking money for Twelfth Step work?" I told him that this issue had been settled long since. Most emphatically I could not, regardless of the consequences, nor could any other AA member. "Well, Bill," said Father Ed, "if you were the only one concerned, you could certainly start wearing a hair shirt and take nothing. But what about Lois? Once upon a time you made a marriage contract to support her. Suppose you put her on the charity of friends so that you can do a service organization job for AA free. Would that be the kind of support your marriage contract called for? I should think the royalties would be the best bet."[149]

Father Ed happened to be the right person for these discernment issues. In his Jesuit tradition, discernment was a gift, passed down to him from Ignatius, the founder of the Jesuits, who had distilled his own struggle with discernment in the Spiritual Exercises.

In his first meeting with Bill, Father Ed discerned from Bill's story that *God was doing something special in Bill.* Bill was not to block this work of God. Father Ed, for his part, was there to point out the movement in Bill and call him to surrender to that plan for AA. This is not the outside "guidance" of the Oxford Group. Dr. Bob's son, Smitty, recalls the problem of "outside guidance."

> I went over to some of the Oxford Group meetings then. In the Oxford Group, you worked the other guy's program for him. You got divine guidance for somebody

else, and they got it for you. Well, you can imagine how that went over with the drunks! Of course, the wives were ready to give this guidance to their husbands at any time, but the drunks sure didn't want any part of it. That was one of the things that made the Oxford Group totally unacceptable to the alcoholics. They got some strange guidance from other people.[150]

Father Ed, on the other hand, called Bill to be open and to surrender to how God was acting *in him,* in his own desires and thirst. Father Ed operated out of a Jesuit presupposition: God can speak in the desires of our hearts.[151] During his eight-day retreat once each year he would pray the Spiritual Exercises of St. Ignatius, which contained both the rules for the discernment of spirits and the rules for discerning God's will.[152]

Discernment was precisely the function Father Ed saw himself doing as he related to AA. When Bill W. asked him to be a trustee for AA, Father Ed wrote his own provincial superior. "I attribute this (the offer of the trusteeship) to a very free use of the Rules for the Discernment of spirits for the second week (Rules one can preach without practicing)."[153] The rules for the second week presupposed a person has chosen the path to God, the path of humility. They have learned the secret of turning humiliations into humility. In this path a person receives God's blessing. The discernment task of this stage is to choose between the good and the better, exactly what Bill talked about in his essay on Tradition Two. Father Ed framed this discernment in the context of detachment in his letter at the end of this book's Chapter 4 when he said, "most spiritual development seems to be not through achievement but detachment."[154]

This movement for greater and greater detachment will find a visual presentation later in the Two Standards meditation. In 1952 Father Ed sent Bill a copy of the Spiritual Exercises. Bill had requested a copy of *The Spiritual Exercises of St. Ignatius* at about the time he was working on the *Twelve Steps and Twelve Traditions.*[155] The Two Standards meditation emphasized detachment and set a framework for discernment: the evil spirit, a battlefield commander on a smoky throne, will try to lead us through riches to pride and from there to all other vices. The good spirit, Christ on a level, lowly plain, will ask us to follow Him through humiliations to humility and from there to all other blessings.[156]

In these Spiritual Exercises, Ignatius by 1525 had distilled his prayer and life experiences into a manual with principles for the spiritual journey. This small book contains what Ignatius had learned the hard way. Someone said the best way to learn discernment is by making mistakes, or as Carl Jung said, "The right way to wholeness is made of fateful detours and wrong turnings." Ignatius literally fell into discernment. He had been knocked down in 1521 by a French cannonball as he defended a castle at Pamplona. During his recovery, doctors cut the bone and stretched his bad leg. Confined to bed, he asked for something to read and hoped it would be romances, the soft porn of his time. All his relatives could find were books on the lives of the saints and the life of Christ.

Without romances, he turned to his own imagination. He found he could imagine for two, three, four hours at a time being in the service of a noble lady and how he would woo her with gallant deeds and verses.

At another time he read the life of Christ or the lives of the saints and would pause to imagine, "Suppose that I should do what St. Francis did, what Dominic did?" He would picture himself like St. Francis or St. Dominic. "They did this, I must do them one better." The God thoughts and worldly thoughts alternated in his mind. Ignatius began to experience a difference in feeling between these two ways of thinking.

> There was, however this difference. When he was thinking of the things of the world he was filled with delight, but when afterwards he dismissed them from weariness, he was dry and dissatisfied. And when he thought of going barefoot to Jerusalem and of eating nothing but herbs and performing the other rigors he saw that the saints had performed, he was consoled, not only when he entertained these thoughts, but even after dismissing them he remained cheerful and satisfied.

But he paid no attention to this, nor did he stop to weigh the difference until one day his eyes were opened a little and he began to wonder at the difference and to reflect on it, learning from experience that one kind of thoughts left him sad and the other cheerful. Thus, step by step, he came to recognize the difference between the two spirits that moved him, the one being from the evil spirit, the other from God.[157]

This experience led to Ignatius becoming more sensitive to his inner movements, his own beginning discernment. At times the discernment was clear; choice followed quickly. Other times the discernment was not clear and only came after a series of mistakes. For example, often Ignatius, while trying to sleep at night, would find himself "flooded by great illuminations and spiritual consolations, which made him lose much of the time he had set aside for sleep, and that was not much." Ignatius reflected this way in his diary.

He looked into this matter a number of times and gave it some thought. Having set aside much time for dealing with God (seven hours in the day) and besides that even all the rest of the day, he began to doubt whether these illuminations came from the good spirit. He concluded that he had better not have anything to do with them, and give the time determined on to sleep. This he did.[158]

Ignatius would write that a person needed to watch the beginning, middle, and end of a thought process: does the movement close us up or lead us to greater openness to others and God? Dowling would quote this principle to Bill when Bill claimed he was helped in writing the *Twelve Steps and Twelve Traditions* by a psychic experience of an 11th century bishop, Boniface.[159] Dowling put this discernment principle in a quote referring to the opening scene and power temptation in *Macbeth,* "These folks sometimes tell us truth in small matters in order to fool us in larger."[160]

Ignatius also warned that the good can sometimes be the

enemy of the best. This discernment area Father Ed claimed as his own gift to AA: the area of choosing between equally good options for those advancing in recovery. Bill faced many discernment issues: the place of money and power in AA, whether AA would be racially exclusive, whether or not Bill would become a Roman Catholic, whether or not to accept the Yale honorary doctorate, whether or not to use LSD.[161] He also faced his own "riches" — security from approval, romance, power — in his 1958 essay, "The New Frontier: Emotional Sobriety."

From this Bill learned to listen to his desires, to be aware of his inner dynamics, and to tune into the action of God in him for the good of AA. Some said he did this very well for AA but not as well in his own life. Doing this meant learning to recognize and identify his personal, spiritual movements: those inner promptings, attractions — often called emotions or affections — which are part of ordinary human experience. This tuning into God's action at one's center is discernment. One of the people who helped Bill grow in discernment, "the wisdom to know the difference," was that Jesuit priest with a cane who limped into the New York AA clubhouse one sleet-filled November night in 1940.

CHAPTER 12

20th Anniversary Celebration: God's Steps to Humanity

Bill trusted the loving care of a higher power for himself and AA. At the 1955 convention, Bill celebrated the fruit of this trust and thanked those who helped AA come of age. The next thirty letters center on the aftermath of the convention, while the first of these letters shows Father Ed looking forward to the convention.[162]

Father Ed wrote Bill on February 21, 1955, that "The first five days of July are marked on my calendar for the convention." In the same letter he told of Father Dan Lord's death. Lord, his friend and boss, had seen Dowling's gifts and called him to The Queen's Work. Dowling remarked to a friend after Lord's wake, "Make sure I am embalmed. I don't want to wake up buried." Dowling, himself, would be dead within five years. Typically, he mentioned the kind of thing he was always doing: working in groups. "I am having a little caucus weekly of non-alcoholics to study the use and integration of the 12 steps and the Spiritual Exercises for everyday affairs."

The next thirty letters cover many levels: the facts of their lives, the graces of the convention, and the retrieval of Father Ed's convention talk for *Alcoholics Anonymous Comes of Age*. On the factual level, Bill was just back from vacation with Lois in Panama and concerned about Father Ed, who with eye problems, was just out of St. John's Hospital. In the fall Bill missed Father Ed when he was in New York for the Summer School of Catholic Action because his mother had arrived unexpectedly. Early in February of 1957, Bill visited St. Louis out of concern for Father Ed's failing health.

In Bill's 1955 Christmas letter he wrote about the convention, now come and gone, "Please know that we shall always see you standing in the forefront of those devoted ranks, of those who have brought us to today."

> Last summer at St. Louis, AA gained another summit on the journey to whatever destiny God may have in store for us. That you have been such a boon companion, wise counselor, and devoted friend to so many, and to Lois and to me, will always be something for our constant affection and gratitude.[163]

Sponsors help each other discern where the hand of God is and help each other claim graces. Father Ed underlined some graces from the convention:

> Last week I saw some figure skaters in St. Paul do the most impossible glides so easily that they gave me the feeling that I could do them myself.
>
> The convention — God's blessing on it — the grateful and generous cooperation with God's Help by so many highly trained people left a like impression that grows as the convention recedes into the past.[164]

Father Ed added in his next letter, "The Convention's landmark quality becomes clearer as time goes on."[165]

Bill, for his part, saw the presentation Lois made at the Convention on the Family Groups (Al-Anon) as both well received and a breakthrough for the total movement. Lois emphasized the spouse of the alcoholic needed to work the same steps in his or her own life and leave the alcoholic free to work his or her own steps. Bill underlined this gift to their marriage of Lois working her program.

> To my mind, one of the happiest events at the convention was the deep impression the Family Group performance made on the AA members. More than ever, I think it is

one of the greatest developments since AA began. In our own house, this has certainly been the case. The effect of this development on Lois and on me has been nothing short of magic.[166]

In his letter of August 2, 1955, Bill wrote of the new structure in the service legacy, which allowed him and Dr. Bob to pass on the authority for AA to the General Service Conference:

I suppose the establishment of the General Service Conference on a permanent basis will be our last venture in prophesy. The AA book and the old Foundation were similar ventures. They had to be set into the functional picture before the average AA realized the need for such things. I hope we will be equally blessed by Providence this last time.

Father Ed, after Bill sent him a rough draft of *Alcoholics Anonymous Comes of Age,* praised Bill's Appendix, "Why AA is Anonymous." "The chapter on anonymity is a classic. It interweaves philosophy and practicality with very real craftsmanship."[167] Bill's opening lines must have struck a sympathetic chord: Bill placed anonymity as the exact opposite of the drive for power, exactly the framework Father Ed had pointed to in the meditation on the Two Standards.

As never before, the struggle for power, importance, and wealth is tearing civilization apart — man against man, family against family, group against group, nation against nation.

Nearly all those engaged in this fierce competition declare that their aim is peace and justice for themselves, their neighbors, and their nations. "Give us power," they say, "and we shall have justice; give us fame and we shall set a great example; give us money and we shall be comfortable and happy." People throughout the world deeply believe such things and act accordingly. On this appalling dry bender, society seems to be staggering down a dead-end road. This stop sign is clearly marked. It says "Disaster."[168]

Bill saw the cure in *self-sacrifice:* of our ambition and illegitimate pride, of our time in Twelve Stepping, of giving ourselves for the common welfare. Bill even told the story of his own hunger for prestige and early anonymity breaks. In his appendix on anonymity Bill offered his own exercise of discernment on anonymity slips and concluded that "the temporary or seeming good can often be the deadly enemy of the permanent best. When it comes to survival for AA, nothing short of our very best will be good enough."[169] Or as Bill wrote in *Twelve Steps and Twelve Traditions,* "We are sure that humility, expressed by anonymity, is the greatest safeguard that Alcoholics Anonymous can ever have." Anonymity is real humility at work.[170] It would seem that the themes of the Ignatian meditation on the Two Standards (the way of humility vs. the way of pride) frame Bill's comments on anonymity.

All these special graces from the convention Bill wanted in a book. He wrote Father Ed:

We think that the St. Louis proceedings ought to be put in a book form so that they can be widely shared by our membership. In this connection, I think the New York Office has already written to you, seeking your permission to use your talk in whole or in part — something of a favor which I trust you will grant.[171]

Father Ed usually spoke from an outline and clippings, which he would hold in his hand like a card player. It was no small thing to retrieve a Dowling talk. Father Ed asked for a transcript of his recorded talk. "I do not usually finish my sentences and I think a transcript might assist me in cutting it down to the brevity necessary."[172]

Bill promised to send a typed copy of the talk from the convention tape and asked Father Ed to shorten his quotes from Thompson's "The Hound of Heaven." Bill wrote, "I wonder whether you would consider cutting down the Thompson a little and putting in more of Father Ed? I feel closer to him anyhow!"[173]

Once Bill had sent him the rough copy for *Alcoholics Anonymous Comes of Age,* Father Ed commented on the book as a whole and offered eighteen suggestions on his own talk. Dowling's talk is remarkable in its explicit Roman Catholic Christianity offered in the steps of God to humanity. In Father Ed's earlier letters, interventions of God were "incarnations."[174] Deflation and humiliation prepared humans for God's interventions; God, Himself, entered this world as a man, enduring deflation and humiliation — even to torture and execution. Dowling put it this way in his talk:

We know AA's Twelve Steps of man toward God. May I suggest God's Twelve Steps toward man as Christianity has taught them to me. The first step is described by St. John. The Incarnation. The word was God and the word became flesh and dwelt amongst us. He turned His life and His will over to the care of man as He understood him. The second step, nine months later, closer to us in the circumstances of it, is the birth, the Nativity. The third step, the next thirty years, the anonymous hidden life. Closer, because it is so much like our own. The fourth step, three years of public life.

The fifth step, His teaching, His example, our Lord's Prayer. The sixth step, bodily suffering, including thirst, on Calvary.

The next step, soul suffering in Gethsemane; that's coming close. How well the alcoholic knows, and how well He knew, humiliation and fear and loneliness and discouragement and futility. Finally death, another step closer to us, and I think the passage where a dying God rests in the lap of a human mother is as far down as divinity can come, and probably the greatest height that humanity can reach.

Down the ages He comes closer to us as head of a sort of Christians Anonymous, a mystical body laced together by His teachings. "Whatsoever you do to the least of these my brethren so do you unto me." "I can fill up what is wanting in the sufferings of Christ." "I was in prison and you visited me." "I was sick and I was hungry and you gave me to eat."

The next step is the Christian Church, which I believe is Christ here today. A great many sincere people say, "I like Christianity, but I don't like Churchianity." I can understand that. I understand it better than you do because I'm involved in Churchianity and it bothers me too! But, actually, I think that sounds a little bit like saying, "I do love good drinking water but I hate plumbing." Now, who does like plumbing? You have people who like sobriety, but they won't take A.A.

And then the eleventh step is several big pipe lines or sacraments of God's help. And the twelfth step, to me, is the great pipe line or sacrament of Communion. The word that was God became flesh and becomes our food, as close to us as the fruit juice and the toast and the coffee we had an hour ago.[175]

The steps of God among us end in the lap of his mother, holding her Son, executed among outcasts, at the foot of the cross. Father Ed continues with "The Hound of Heaven," a poem by an outcast, a narcotic addict, Francis Thompson. This poem described a person fleeing God across the face of the earth and trying to find happiness everywhere except in God. And God — as the Hound of Heaven — follows until they finally talk.

> All which I took from thee I did but take,
> Not for thy harms,
> But just that thou mightst seek it in My arms.
> All which thy child's mistake
> Fancies as lost, I have in stored for thee at home:
> Rise, clasp My hand, and come!

Father Ed ends with the alcoholic answering:

> Is my gloom, after all,
> The shade of His hand, outstretched caressingly?
> God replies:
> Ah, fondest, blindest, weakest,
> I am He Whom thou seekest![176]

Both the steps of God to man and the "Hound of Heaven" raised the outcast to the same path God chose: suffering and humiliation. Father Ed in the same talk quoted Bernard Smith, then Chairman of AA Trustees, "The tragedy of our life is how deep must be our suffering before we learn the simple truths by which we can live."[177]

The addict cannot escape the depth of suffering; God freely chose suffering as an outcast among outcasts the place of humiliation and blessing.

In his talk, Father Ed spoke as one caught up in the way God stepped down to earth and today continues with interventions (incarnations) to meet other outcasts. These interventions, marked by suffering and humility, are "This hand outstretched caressingly," hands pierced on the cross.

This might explain Bill's choice of Father Ed's picture for *Alcoholics Anonymous Comes of Age.* In the picture, Father Ed, wiping his glasses with his crumpled handkerchief, stands in front of the cross at his Queen's Work office. Anna Dowling sent that same cross to Bill, along with her brother's cane, after Father Ed's death. Both found a place of honor in Bill's studio, Wit's End. The cane was to the right of his fireplace; Dowling's cross, a little to the right above the fireplace mantel. Bill wrote to Anna thanking her, "I am sure that Ed's crucifix and his cane are the finest mementos — indeed, relics — of him that anybody could possess.... I look at these wonderful objects that mean so much to me — and to so many. They will find a resting place on a wall of my studio — the only place where I can be alone."[178]

Dowling once celebrated this love for the suffering Christ when he said, "The two marks of a thoroughbred are that he never refuses a jump and that he is a good mud runner. Both are impossible without closeness to the suffering Christ."[179] Dowling once wrote to a student's mother who had suffered a stroke, "I don't know or understand your suffering, but I do know the love that honors you in your suffering."

Dowling, the good mud runner who never refused a jump, knew the place where love meets suffering.

CHAPTER 13

A Softer, Easier Way:
the LSD Experiment

At the 1955 AA Convention, Father Ed had focused on God's steps to humankind. Father Ed often pointed to God's steps in Bill's life as he did at their first meeting, "God's hand is here, go with God." From his conversion experience at Towns Hospital, Bill knew that deflation comes before an experience of God.

Some letters in this chapter show Father Ed gently calling Bill to discernment about his LSD experiments. Bill felt the experiments were a way to lower defenses—a kind of chemical deflation—so that God might be experienced more quickly. Bill was looking for anything to lessen suffering and speed recovery, especially for the chronic alcoholic not yet reached by AA.

Father Ed cautioned him with "the good can often be the enemy of the best," and quoted from *Macbeth* that seeming good spirits can tempt us to our woe. The witches in *Macbeth* led him to kill the king, Duncan, by "predicting that he would beget kings" and that he would be the "Thane of Cawdor."[180] This discernment about using LSD would be central among many topics treated in these letters (1958-1960), which coincided with the last two years of Father Ed's life.

One topic: health. Bill wrote after the death of his sister that he was just back from the west coast and had brought his mother, who had suffered a stroke, home. Except for lack of balance, she would be walking about soon. In Father Ed's May 8, 1958, letter, he let Bill know that like Bill's mother, he had had two small strokes. He was praying for Bill's sister and mother. Bill thanked him.[181]

Father Ed's weight continued to be a health problem. He wrote that Bill and Lois needed to start "Obese Obvious" for him. He said he would like to be the first vice president. In the same letter Father Ed wanted Lois to know the many good things he was hearing about Al-Anon. "Obese Obvious" did not start in time.[182] Bill wrote to Joe Diggles, a former student of Father Ed's. "He has recently been here, by the way. He has had a heart attack only a month since; nevertheless he carries on as usual. I think he is one of the great men of our time — a genuine saint."[183]

The following December Father Ed was hospitalized for eight days, and only with the help of a portable oxygen tank was he able to travel to New York for Bill's sobriety anniversary. In April of 1960 Father Ed would die in his sleep of a heart attack.

Another theme the letters touched was asking Bill to surrender to what God was doing in him. Father Ed had asked the same of Bill in their first meeting. These reflections start with a letter to Father Ed from Bill. Father Ed had written to Tom Powers, a writer who had just published a book. Bill said of him, "He [Tom] is a great friend, and I have known few who have tried harder to live according to their lights than he — something I can't claim for myself." Tom's book about spirituality triggered further comment from Bill:

> I expect too, that I'm too complacent, theologically speaking. The immense array of views which are around — views which so often cut off communication between good people — are interesting, but not too important speculations. At least, so it seems. In some ways I feel very close to conservative Christianity. In other respects — important ones to Christians — no particular convictions seem to come. Maybe down deep I don't want to be convinced — I just don't know.[184]

Father Ed responded, "Your feeling of closeness to conservative Christianity without particular conviction of course interests me. From my bigoted perspective it sometimes looks like an alcoholic feels very close to conservative A.A." Father Ed goes on, "But he does not want to be convinced. Christianity Anonymous could be as appalling as Alcoholics Anonymous."[185]

The distinction seems to be that neither Christianity nor AA are worth it unless a person is willing to "walk the talk." Otherwise, it's all talk, no action.

Bill reflected more in his next letter on how so many people of good will can hold different religious beliefs and claimed this might come from his own egotism and upbringing.

How does a fellow like me make up his mind what is right and who is right? While it may well be suspected that this is an alibi for failing to completely adopt the Catholic point of view, it still seems like a good question to which I consciously do not know the answer.

It is certainly uncomfortable to be unsure about many matters of high importance. The only worse fate would be to become cocksure and then turn out to be dead wrong. Or wouldn't it? Honestly, Ed, I really don't know.[186]

In his next letter Father Ed offered—almost as if quoting from class notes—a long reflection on the different kinds of certitude. By the end he is pure Dowling and asked—as he always did—that Bill follow his own truth.

Absolute cocksureness is not the mark of the faith of the Christian. "Lord, I believe, help Thou my unbelief." "Lord, to whom shall we turn?" "Blessed are they who have not seen and have believed."

The best road to truth is suggested by Christ. "Dwell in My way and you will know the truth."

This does not involve doing much different than you are doing. But it means that we should do those things better, more unselfishly. Because I believe that you are doing this—stumblingly, as Christ Himself did—you possess much of that promised truth and are possessed by it.[187]

For Father Ed, Christ stumbled on the way of the cross. Father Ed sees Bill on this way: possessed by truth, stumbling. It was enough. After Father Ed visited Bill that August in New York, he wrote, "You mentioned some interest in the Christian theory of

Baptism of Desire. I am enclosing an excerpt that I ran across. I say Christian because this doctrine prevailed long before the Reformation. It was and is always good to see you."[188]

The enclosed excerpt on "Baptism of Desire" by P.E. Hallett said: If a person has the necessary good disposition to love God and do what is right and cannot be baptized, this person may be saved through this implicit desire for baptism. In a letter to Joe Diggles, Bill mentioned that for him to become a Catholic would be seen as an endorsement of Catholicism. He could not do this: his private person was still identified with his public person.[189]

Sometimes Bill referred to his relationship with the Catholic Church as a "fellow traveler." Father Ed had been consistent in calling Bill to follow his special star, his own vocation before God. Perhaps this is the greatest gift friends give: calling each other to who they are — before God.

The next group of letters cover the LSD experiments, another key discernment issue. Bill knew of finding God through deflation through suffering. Could this process be speeded up through a chemical lowering of defenses, even if just for a short time? Nell Wing mentions in *Grateful to Have Been There* that Bill's friend Gerald Heard introduced him to two English psychiatrists, Drs. Humphrey Osmond and Abram Hoffer, who were using LSD with schizophrenics and alcoholic patients at a Canadian hospital. This was before LSD became a street drug and before government regulations. The psychiatrists reported that the drug was beneficial to their patients, especially in shortening their resistance to treatment. Nell Wing wrote that Bill became enthusiastic about the potential and said, "Anything that helps alcoholics is good and shouldn't be dismissed out of hand."[190]

Bill wrote December 29, 1958, to thank Father Ed for his birthday letter and for launching the "Be kind to Bill Wilson Week" with his homemade birthday card. He went on to wonder about Father Ed's health. Father Ed had just been to New York for Bill's sobriety anniversary and had had to carry a portable oxygen tank. "Quite selfishly I find I am always wishing I could see more of you. I really need your prayers and advice."

Then Bill reflected on his own LSD experiment.

On the psychic front, the LSD business goes on apace.... However, I don't believe that it has any miraculous property of transforming spiritually and emotionally sick people into healthy ones overnight. It can set up a shining goal on the positive side, and on the negative, analytical side it can quickly get to where the trouble is. These things I have repeatedly seen, and to this extent the material can be beneficial. But unless the theologians and psychiatrists wish to make an issue of it, I do not see how the material can seriously upset their own thinking or methods. After all, it is only a temporary ego-reducer. The object of development seems to get the ego down so it will stay that way.

But the vision and insights given by LSD could create a larger incentive — at least in a considerable number of people.

Bill's expectations seem measured as he takes in as much as he can to make his own judgments about LSD. In 1942 he knew that when facing a decision, he had to keep "all channels open." Yet for some in AA, Bill's channels were too open. In an October 26, 1959, letter he wrote Father Ed:

The LSD business created some commotion and this one even more among my friends. The story is "that Bill takes one pill to see God and another to quiet his nerves." No amount of factual information can seem to dispel their fearful doubts. Though one does not like to disturb unnecessarily one's friends, it must be confessed that these recent heresies of mine do have their comic aspect.

About a month later, Bill wrote, "How deeply Lois and I have been affected by your trek to New York to be with us on my Anniversary." Bill added that many had experienced Father Ed as "so warm and full of faith" that if he just counted to one thousand that would be as good as a talk. "That's what you mean to us, Ed; your friendship and example are just treasured things — the finest experience I shall ever know."[191]

Father Ed must have responded in a letter stating his cautions about LSD.[192] Bill answered:

Please be sure that I am very glad that you set out your apprehension about the LSD business. I should have mentioned that two members of our LSD group—have come to share your concern. G. had quite a negative reaction the second time he tried the material. He saw devils and had a deep sense of malignancy. With only one exception, this is the only case I have ever heard of where there was such a development. Under LSD, a delinquent kid, a real bad boy, had a similar experience. Whether such views are to be construed as helpful or damaging is hard to say. If the LSD business is actually invested with malignancy, I would think it likely to be more subtle than this.[193]

Bill continued in the letter to make his case by examining some Native Americans and their use of mescaline in their ceremonies. He found little evidence of evil effects.

According to *Pass It On,* Father Ed had met Bill's LSD group and had been part of an experiment.[194] This would explain what Bill wrote next in this same letter.

The group which you saw in operation was disbanded early this year, partly because the extension of it would have led to a lot of controversy, partly because there was little or no urge on the part of its members to return to the experience, having once had it, and partly because T and G didn't care to go on.[195]

Am enclosing you some notes that were taken on my only experience with the group. These notes are a series of exclamations that I made usually between long pauses in which there was a tremendous inner experience.

As I reread these jottings, the experiences somewhat come back. As I read and remember, it is hard for me to believe this episode to have been either phony or malign. While these notes were fragmentary and a bit unrelated, they do seem to reflect the mediation of quality and they do seem to be theologically in fair order, so far as they go. Maybe you can see something else in these, and if so, I wish you could find time to drop me a line about this.

Since that last group experience, just described, I have early in this year, tried out the material again. These later results were far less of emotional intensity. They varied from the sensations of being at a retreat, to a day of sunny satisfaction at the shore, or to the joys of picnics in fine mountain scenery. Therefore there seems to be a tendency for the emotional context to subside. This had become true when I entered the experience of September 20th. Even this one didn't compare with the great cataclysm, resembling my earlier experience, which took place on the Coast when I first took the material.

But, as I said, there isn't the slightest disposition to rush back into these experiences, or to push them upon anybody else.[196]

In this letter Bill mentioned twice he wanted to know what Father Ed thought of the experiments. Father Ed wrote back on December 14, 1959, that he had been in the hospital for nine days because a "conservative doctor" said he had "over extended."

The rest of this letter is worth quoting because it shows Dowling as sponsor, both underlining the positive and warning about LSD precisely in terms of the discernment rules for the second week of the Ignatian Spiritual Exercises.

So much of the good, the true and the beautiful in the September 20, 1958, transcript.[197] That fact, plus your psycho-sensitivity, plus loss of will control at a stage, plus the proved value of psychic experiment, PLUS the Devil's shrewd malignancy ("Thane of Cawdor — Thane of Glamis...") Jesuit theory makes me cautious in these matters — possibly more cautious than prudent.[198]

St. Ignatius, in his "Rules for Discernment of Spirits" said:

"It is the mark of the evil spirit to assume the appearance of the angel of light. He begins by suggesting thoughts suited to a devout soul but ends by suggesting his own... little by little drawing the soul into his snares and evil designs."

With centuries of time at his disposal the Devil (like a broker) is a percentage player. He will settle for a lesser good — fearing that the greater good might turn out to be another Assisi.[199]

Letting me share your 25 milestone was a peak in the high plateau of my AA-hood. Please tell Lois I am so grateful to her for having my nephew, Paul, to lunch with you. It will be something for him to tell his grandchildren.

You and Lois will be in my Christmas prayers. For the New Year I borrow Thompson's wish that there be no darkness for you but "the shade of His hand outstretched caressingly."[200]

Bill slowed down his LSD experiments and later disbanded the group. He did so because the experiences were less intense, members of the group did not want to continue, and he was scandalizing some of the AA membership.

The "shade of His hand" would appear in an unexpected place: the letters Bill wrote about conflicts in AA.

This year, for the first time, the Conference had three or four good fights, ranging all the way from whether the hotel was a flea-bag to the question of whether a majority of alcoholics could be trusted on the General Service Board to handle our affairs. As you know we have always had a majority of "nons."[201]

Previous to the Conference, I had sent a memorandum to the groups, pointing out that the majority of "nons" was quite appropriate to our infancy and adolescence. Now that period had been passed....This evoked a storm of protest and fear which was most interesting and not a little amazing. The folks back home still seem to think that we'd be safer with eight non-alcoholic policemen to keep the seven drunks in line! and this, despite the fact that all of them are strictly accountable to the Conference itself which looks over our affairs with a microscope each year....

Then there was a letter from Florida which one of the delegates was under instruction to read to the Conference. It was a sizzling affair which blew me and practically all my works to smithereens. It was triggered by the Trustee-ratio controversy and some other considerations. Compared with the fisticuffs we used to have when all of the middle West was against New York and me, it was a very mild matter, practically a flea-bite. But the Delegates didn't see it that way, they were red-hot.

Then they got scared. They thought the Conference was going to fall apart. They much deplored its lack of decorum.

So I took this as an occasion to point out that all of our evolution had been based upon the pressure of our troubles pushing us. Once pushed, God could then draw us. Therefore, the Conference fracasing was perfectly healthy. There was also the assurance that our Conference, notwithstanding these events, had been far better behaved than the average parliamentary body throughout the world. So I believe they went away comforted.[202]

Bill concluded that "our Conference can stand any amount of nonsense and an awful lot of pressure. It was a grand test." Bill showed detachment from the conflict. This was not only a "grand test" for the Conference, but for Bill and his ability to trust both the Conference and God.

That kind of freedom and detachment helped Bill be free to attend to organizational principles. He would not get caught in petty conflicts. In December of that same year he wrote to Father Ed:

Just now I am engaged in doing a series of twelve essays to run underneath Twelve Principles of World Service. The effect will be to make an addition to our Third Legacy Manual of World Service, which just now is mostly procedural. The procedural part tells you "how," but the essay part will tell the "why." It will be an attempt to interpret the procedural part in terms of the history and philosophy of the service structure.[203]

That trust would prepare him for what was to happen next: Father Ed's death.

CHAPTER 14

Dowling's Last Night with Cana and AA

Father Ed had been asked to speak at the AA International Convention in Long Beach, California. He had accepted to speak on "God as we understand Him" for the morning of Sunday, July 3, 1960. Anna Dowling wrote to the coordinator of the Convention that her brother was in the hospital but would be in his office soon and would like to know how long his talk should be.[204]

The convention chairman wrote back to let Dowling know Bill W. would be there as chairman of the Sunday concluding session, as well as Sam Shoemaker. A week later Father Ed learned his talk was to be thirty minutes long. Later, Father Ed wrote, asking for a screen and slide projector to go with his talk, and included his biographical sheet.[205] This was to be his last letter.

Early on Sunday morning, April 3, Father Ed died peacefully in his sleep. He had flown to Memphis, Tennessee, to give a Cana Conference. Bill W. put it this way.

> Unmindful of his ebbing health, he was visiting one of his "Cana" Groups. Never had there been a gayer evening in the hours before; he would have wanted to take his leave in just his way.[206] So passed on one of the most gentle souls and one of the finest friends that we AA's may ever know. He left a heritage of inspiration and Grace that will be with us always.

Father Ed had planned to be at our 1960 Long Beach Convention, come July. This prospect now to be unfulfilled, brings the recollection of his appearance at AA's St. Louis International Convention of 1955. It seems altogether fitting that I repeat the introduction that I then made of him, together with an account of the unforgettable impression he left upon me the very first time we met—a fragment of history recorded in *A.A. Comes of Age.*[207]

Then Bill told again the story of the bum from St. Louis who walked in out of the sleet one November night in 1940—and the man who brought peace and the gift of discernment.

Paul K. of Memphis wrote to a friend, Lyb, in St. Louis about not being able to get time off from work to come into St. Louis for the funeral. He went on to say he was among those with Father Ed that last night in Memphis.

But I can't complain. Luckier than Bill W. in this case, I shared his last evening on earth and yesterday at the Funeral Home I had the last hour alone with him and then rode down with him to the train.

To go back: knowing he was coming I had written to him at the Queen's Work and asked for a few minutes of his time. His reply came promptly giving his local address and that he was coming in Saturday afternoon. I had hoped to have him for dinner with a few of our friends whom you and Hank met here.

After his arrival he phoned me that it had gotten a trifle crowded and could I come out after dinner. I told him to let it ride, Sunday would do. In his letter he had mentioned that he had been recently hospitalized with a cardiac condition. But he sounded so disappointed that I said I'd be glad to come—and for that will I ever be eternally grateful.

I took an AA Gal (3 years) with me and he was very glad to show us off; the others belonged to the Cana Conferences he had originated and he wanted to emphasize how AA's faced their problems and spoke about problems and about "God directly and not as if the word were immodest like 'legs' in the Victorian age." The quotes are direct.

We left saying we'd see him on Sunday but, as you know, he had a higher engagement. One look at him and I knew he wouldn't be with us long; he left us as he would have liked — among friends he loved and who loved him — and with AA the night before. Those in the Fellowship were always his "pets" so to speak — you could tell that by the way his eyes lit up when we came in the room.

For Bill's sake I am glad that Father Ed's passing was so peaceful...this departure out of our sight was fitting and in keeping with Father Ed's life and wishes.

I'm still a bit numb but comforted by the fact that I have another friend at court — and I'll need all I can get.[208]

Father Ed once defended contemplative orders to Dr. Bob by saying, "Trafficking with God in prayer is pretty high society and a very influential social activity." He concluded, "these people are our lobbyists before the divine legislature."[209] Dowling's death just changed his workplace and job title from "God's ambassador to humanity" to "lobbyist before the throne of God."

The Jesuit pastor did not want the funeral to be at the College Church, St. Francis Xavier's. He suggested Father Ed be buried from The Queen's Work, really just an office building. The provincial (higher superior) intervened and ordered that Father Ed be buried out of the College Church. Father Fred Zimmerman, manager for The Queen's Work, handled the details of the funeral. Later, he wrote, "When we gathered near the grave at Florissant, Father Leo Brown next to me remarked, 'So this is the man they would not bury from the College Church?' The cemetery and the grounds were packed with cars and people who came from all over the country. Mr. Wilson was there to give Puggy Dowling a sendoff that was rarely seen at Florissant. To distract Anna Dowling, I made her call all the Jesuit houses in the Province from St. Mathew's rectory."[210]

The editor of the St. John's Hospital Newsletter says that in her pew at the funeral there was a little old lady rattling a paper lunch bag who cried throughout the whole funeral mass.

The argument over the place of funeral suggests those Jesuits who thought their intellectual or parish ministry was more mainstream; Father Ed's on the fringe. He had lived with these judgments during his life — not without suffering, not without humor, not without grace. He had played well in the ballpark of suffering. As he wrote on the book jacket for *Alcoholics Anonymous*, "God resists the proud, assists the humble. The shortest cut to humility is humiliations, which AA has in abundance." He often quoted to Bill W. the scripture, "In My Father's house there are many mansions." He had lived his truth, in good times and bad, to the place from which all blessings flow, the house with many mansions.

Conclusion:
A Ballpark Named Recovery

Father Ed, speaking of suffering, quoted from Whittaker Chambers, "And yet it is at this very point that man, that monstrous midget, still has the edge on the Devil. He suffers. Not one man, however base, quite lacks the capacity for the specific suffering which is the seal of his divine commission."[211]

That divine commission, suffering — arthritis and overeating for Father Ed, alcoholism and depression for Bill — became tickets into a special ballpark: recovery. Both men believed in a democracy of people helping through mutual vulnerability. To keep this healing, they gave it away, hand-to-hand, circle-to-circle. That the circle might hold for the next suffering alcoholic, Bill crafted the traditions with leadership "on tap, not on top."

Father Ed once campaigned to change the game of baseball for television. He wanted the diamond to be round so the camera could follow the players more easily. Bill turned the AA ball diamond upside down by choosing poverty and anonymity over power and riches. In recovery Bill detached from his own riches: approval, romance, and honors. Father Ed happened to be one of those who pointed to humility as the place of discerning choice and blessing.

Bill knew Father Ed's own vision of Steps Six and Seven as the way of the suffering Christ. Father Ed had claimed this understanding both in his 1955 Convention talk and in his suggestions for *Twelve Steps and Twelve Traditions*. The paradox of suffering, death to life, that Father Ed saw in Steps Six and Seven had been the very paradox of "suffering leading to regeneration" that led Father Ed to Bill that first November night in 1940.

This paradox found visualization in the "Meditation on the Two Standards," with one leader's call to riches and power, the other leader's call to humiliations as blessings. These choices formed teams: one for death, the other for life. This second team Father Ed would praise in the words Bill chose for the jacket of the Big Book, "God resists the proud, assists the humble. The shortest cut to humility is humiliations, which AA has in abundance." Father Ed, as sponsor, would call Bill to make choices from that place and trust the care of God — for himself and for the whole of AA.

The rest of what Bill chose for the Big Book jacket blurb from Father Ed is just as telling. "The achievements of AA, which grew out of this book, are profoundly significant. Non-alcoholics should read the last eight words of the 12th step." With those words, "to practice these steps in all our affairs," Father Ed opened the ballpark of recovery to those suffering from other addictions.

That made the ballpark big enough for the world and a whole new ballgame with more players, more laughter — because Bill had welcomed in from the cold a "bum from St. Louis," a ballplayer who would go to bat for AA. And they became friends.

Endnotes

[1] Although Alcoholics Anonymous remains carefully cautious about the anonymity of even its deceased members, the Fellowship, as well as G.S.O. practice, with the approval of the families concerned, have for over a decade used the full names of AA's co-founders.

[2] Letter from Bill W. to King McElroy, June 14, 1966.

[3] Letter from Bill W. to Anna Dowling, June 1, 1961.

[4] Robert Thomsen, *Bill W.* (New York: Harper Colophon, 1985). This and the next two books are my primary sources for AA history: Ernest Kurtz, *Not God* (Center City: Hazelden, 1979) and *Pass It On* (New York: A.A. World Services, Inc., 1984). This first chapter relies on Thomsen's *Bill W.*, 298-310.

[5] See Appendix E for a list of the Twelve Steps.

[6] Thomsen, 309. Father Ed's calling Bill to the "force that is all his own" comes from Thomsen's book, based on his own interviews with Bill W. Bill told the story of meeting Father Ed at the 1955 convention and had told it earlier in a talk at Le Moyne College (Jesuit) in Syracuse, N.Y., in April 1954.

[7] *Alcoholics Anonymous* (often simply called *The Big Book*) 8-10.

[8] See Dowling's "Proportional Representation" in *Father Dowling Remembered,* Fall 1985, ed., Mary Lou Adams, 23-28. "Proportional Representation" is a method to give all voters a more complete expression of their wishes in selecting people for office. As recently as April 1993, *Blueprint for*

Social Justice in an article by Douglas Amy, "When Every Vote Counts," agrees with Dowling, that minorities would have more voice in elections with PR.

[9] Thomsen, *Bill W.,* 40.

[10] As we will see in his June 20, 1952, letter to Bill about the Two Standards meditation in the *Spiritual Exercises of St. Ignatius,* Dowling holds up *humility* as a place for choosing for life. At this time he sent Bill a copy of *The Spiritual Exercises.* This is in contrast to the Oxford Group, who sought out prominent persons for converts. Mel B. points this out in his book, *New Wine: The Spiritual Roots of the Twelve Step Miracle* (Center City: Hazelden, 1991), 30, 149.

[11] *Pass It On,* 24.

[12] Ernest Kurtz, *Not God* (Center City: Hazelden, 1975), 10.

[13] *Pass It On,* 25.

[14] Bill Pittman, *A.A. The Way It Began* (Seattle: Glen Abbey Books, 1988), 143.

[15] Bill Pittman, *A.A. The Way It Began,* 144.

[16] *Pass It On,* 36.

[17] Bill Wilson, "The Next Frontier—Emotional Sobriety," in *The Language of the Heart* (New York: The AA Grapevine, Inc., 1988), 236-242. Bill's own explanation of his depression differs from the interpretation in *Pass It On,* which sees Bill being free from depression when he could let his control of the fellowship go at the 1955 convention (303). Nell Wing notes that Bill did not really let go until 1962 and that his depression lasted from 1945 to 1955. Nell credits Vitamin B3 with helping Bill out of depression.

[18] *Pass It On,* 40.

[19] *Pass It On,* 60. Bill reports this same sense of peace in his first meeting with Father Ed.

[20] *Pass It On,* 67.

[21] For a good discussion of the Oxford Group's relation to AA, see Mel B.'s *New Wine: The Spiritual Roots of the Twelve Step Miracle* (Center City: Hazelden, 1991), 27ff.

[22] AA's first friend from the world of medicine who treated Bill and first gave knowledge of the disease as a "physical allergy plus mental obsession." *Alcoholics Anonymous Comes of Age,* 13, 52, 63, 67.

[23] Thomsen, 230.

[24] Estha Jones remembered this map in a newsletter for St. John's Hospital the month of Father Ed's death, April 1960. She made it clear she lived in the "booby belt."

[25] Rhea Felknor, "Glad Gethsemane, The Story of Father Edward Dowling, S.J.," *Voice of St. Jude,* June 1960, 14-19. Felknor suggests that, had Father Ed faced Cromwell, he would for the same reason have received the same fate.

[26] Story told to Jim Egan by Mary Lou Adams, in charge of Dowling Archives at Maryville College.

[27] Bill W. speaks of his similar detachment from the Santa Claus God in his commentary on Step Two in the *Twelve Steps and Twelve Traditions,* 31. Father Ed's talk is in the Dowling Archives, Maryville College.

[28] He would distill the wisdom from his suffering in an article for The Queen's Work called, "How to Enjoy Being Miserable." See Appendix B. This wisdom frequently found its way into letters to Ruth Thome, and to Mrs. Dingles, the mother of Joe, a student he taught at Ignatius.

[29] Dowling Archives.

[30] The intellectuals and the also-rans.

[31] Daniel A. Lord, S.J., *Played by Ear* (Chicago: Loyola University Press, 1955), 163.

[32] From an interview with Father Ben Fulkerson, S.J., by Father Jim Egan, S.J., July 1986. He was a founding member of the American Newspaper Guild and remained close to newsmen all his life.

[33] "Glad Gethsemane, The Story of Father Edward Dowling, S.J.," by Rhea Felknor in *The Voice of St. Jude,* Fall 1960. This last interview with Father Ed has good material on the Cana movement.

[34] Jim Egan's interview with Barnaby Faherty, June 1986.

[35] November 1958 letter to Frank Riley.

[36] Letter of January 7, 1985, from James McQuade to Jim Egan.

[37] In a letter from Mary Wehner of January 7, 1985, to Jim Egan. Father Ed Started Cana (Couples Are Not Alone) in 1944 as help for families. This family group used the Twelve Steps.

[38] Father Jim Egan, S.J., interview July 1986 with Father Chimanatto, S.J. Father Ed fired off words in short shots and had been used several times in public debates against Father Lord to show both sides of a question. Father Bill Wade, S.J., a master of argument and humor, filled this role too with Father Lord in public debates. Three heavy hitters.

[39] Mary Weher in a letter to Jim Egan on January 7, 1985.

[40] In the early days of television the camera covered only the batter, pitcher, and play, not the whole diamond.

[41] In a letter from Father Jim Swetnan, S.J., of June 5, 1990, to the author. Dowling wrote the commissioner of baseball about his results. No reply is on record.

[42] Robert Bellah used baseball as a metaphor to understand institutions in his book, *The Good Society* (New York: Vintage Books, 1992), 38-42. Dowling delighted in forming groups where people could be "wounded healers" for each other. All his life he was a grassroots advocate of widespread local participation in politics, believing proportional representation was a way to guarantee oppressed groups some political representation. He was a champion of PR to the end of his life. Sam Lambert, "Father Ed Dowling," *The Jesuit Bulletin*, Oct. 1970, 13.

[43] Interview by author with John G. Scott, March 18, 1993.

[44] December 7, 1945.

[45] A good discussion of Bill's search for God both in psychic phenomena as well as in Catholic doctrine is found in Chapter 16 of *Pass It On* (New York: Alcoholics Anonymous World Services, 1984), 275-285. Official Catholic doctrine discouraged communication with spirits from the otherworld.

[46] Same letter from Dowling archives, December 7, 1945.

[47] Father La Buffe had been on the staff of the Jesuit national magazine *America* and trained street corner preachers for New York's Columbus Circle. He would listen to them to be sure they said the right thing. The two books are *Spiritism and Religion* by John Liljencrants, and *The Dangers of Spiritualism* by J. Godfrey Raupert. Both of these books are in what Bill called the "Spook

Room," in the first floor right off the living room at Stepping Stones. Here, Bill and his friends conducted psychic experiments.

[48] Chapter 11, "Is This God Speaking?" of this book has further examples of discernment.

[49] "Dry bender" was an early term in AA circles to describe what is now called a "dry drunk." The alcoholic has stopped drinking but not "stinking thinking" (resentments and self-pity). Dowling called Bill to AA's Second Step, "Came to believe a power greater than ourselves could restore us to sanity." Bill knew gratitude to God was one quick way to snap a "dry bender." Bill referred to Father Ed as his "spiritual sponsor" (see Introduction). In "Another Fragment of History" (*Grapevine*, February 1954, 2-5), Bill W. credits the Cleveland-Akron groups with developing "organized personal sponsorship." For a fine reflection of how Bill W. used sponsors see pp. 207-8 of Ernest Kurtz and Katherine Ketcham's *The Spirituality of Imperfection* (New York: Bantam, 1992)

[50] Ignatius distilled his conversion and prayer experiences in a little book called *The Spiritual Exercises*. Through this book he offered others a way to discern spirits and contact God. The Spanish Inquisition put him in prison for offering these since he was only a layman with no formal theology. He was subsequently vindicated by the Church.

[51] Bill's obedience to group conscience is clear in the story he tells in *Alcoholics Anonymous Comes of Age* about the group that would not let him be a paid alcoholism counselor at Towns, 99-102.

[52] Dowling had taken Dismas as his vow name in the Jesuits, the name of the thief who asked Jesus on the cross to remember him when he came into his kingdom. Clark had changed his name to Dismas in his ministry to Missouri prisons and founding a half-way house for ex-cons in an old schoolhouse in St. Louis. The story of Father Dismas Clark was featured in a movie called *The Hoodlum Priest* and told in Elizabeth Mulligan's *Hoodlum Priest* (St. Louis: Sunrise Publications, 1979).

[53] Letter from Dowling to Wilson, February 18, 1942.

[54] Daniel M. O'Connell, S.J., "The Grace of God Still Needed in Sure Cures for Alcoholics" (*America*, February 14, 1942), 514-515. O'Connell did some good reading from Dr. Silkworth, the Jack Alexander *Saturday Evening Post* article, and consulted with AA members. He insists on grace and the power of God as only a priest speaking from the outside of a movement can. Dowling had him right.

[55] Dr. Bob Smith, AA's co-founder from Akron, Ohio.

[56] *Pass It On,* 273-4.

[57] Another Jesuit, Father John Ford, S.J., a leading moral theologian, related to AA in both these roles as ambassador and interpreter. He also wrote a book on alcoholism, *Man Takes a Drink.* Ford was the thinker and more for authority *from hierarchy*; Dowling, the pastor and for authority *from the people.* See Ford's introduction to Mary Darrah's *Sister Ignatia, Angel of AA* (Chicago: Loyola University Press, 1992).

[58] See Chapter 9 in this book, "The Spiritual Exercises and the Traditions."

[59] Ignatius, the founder of the Jesuits, asked those in prayer to pray out of their *desires* as a place where God's will would be revealed. Rev. Harry Fosdick, a Riverside Church minister Bill knew, would refer to praying out of "dominant desire." See Edward Kinerk's "Eliciting Great Desires: Their Place in the Spirituality of the Society of Jesus" (*Studies in the Spirituality of Jesuits,* November 1984, Vol. XVI, No. 5).

[60] A quick summary of Lord's summer school style is in Peter McDonough's *Men Astutely Trained* (New York: The Free Press, 1992), 86-89.

[61] McQuade Letter to Jim Egan, October 4, 1984.

[62] 2218 First Avenue South, Minneapolis.

[63] Bill's letter, March 20, 1943.

[64] A. Poulain, S.J., *The Graces of Interior Prayer* (St. Louis: B. Herder Book Co., 1910). The book deals with discerning both the pitfalls and steps to receive God's visitations in mystical prayer.

[65] In earlier letters Dowling had sent another of his favorite books to Bill, Bruce Marshall's *Father Malachy's Miracle.* Dowling noted in his July 15, 1942, letter, "glad you liked *Father Malachy's Miracle.*" This book is a cute presentation of a miracle worked for a struggling church with a laugh at the skeptics. Father Malachy moves by prayer the local dance hall, "The Garden of Eden," to a remote island. The point of the book is clear: God can intervene in history. See Chapter 8 of this book on God's interventions provoked by Bill's argument against infallibility.

[66] March 16, 1944. The cross-country trip lasted from October 24, 1943, until January 1944.

[67] *Pass It On,* 287.

[68] Chapter 18 of *Pass It On* describes well the depth and length of Bill's depression.

[69] Letter from Bill to Henry J. September 22, 1953. The letters in this chapter are from the AA file on the letters Bill wrote to those suffering from depression. Some were in AA, others not.

[70] *As Bill Sees It* (New York: AA General Service Conference, 1967). Letter, 1960, 92.

[71] This was especially true of Bill's commentary on Step Eleven. His finding the "prayer of St. Francis" let him break through to others and eventually to relief from depression. See also Bill's last letter in this chapter, in which he speaks of "outgoing love" as related to recovery from depression.

[72] Personal interview with Nell Wing, March 5, 1991.

[73] Bill as the first pioneer in recovery faced recovery issues in the "purple haze" without the maps of today for the recovery journey, such as Earnie Larsen's *Stage II Recovery* (San Francisco: Harper & Row, 1985), or the *First, Second, and Third Year Sobriety* books by Guy Kettelhack (San Francisco: Harper, 1992).

[74] Bill to Harry Jones of Detroit, September 22, 1953. Bill's use of the words "neurosis" and "absolute dependency" referring to his drive for approval and glory seem to come from the first chapter, "The Search For Glory," he had read in Karen Horney's *Neurosis and Human Growth* (New York: W.W. Norton & Company, 1950).

[75] July 29, 1946.

[76] Nell Wing, *Grateful to Have Been There* (Chicago: Parkside Publishing, 1992), 53.

[77] Baseball contains this paradox of our culture: success next to failure. Francis Vincent, former commissioner of baseball said: "Baseball teaches us...how to deal with failure. We learn at a very young age that failure is the norm in baseball and precisely because we have failed, we hold in high regard those who fail less often — those who hit safely in one out of three chances and become star players. I also find it fascinating that baseball alone in sport, considers errors to be part of the game, part of its rigorous truth." Ernest Kurtz in the introduction to his book *The Spirituality of Imperfection* (New York: Bantam, 1992) quotes Vincent from his article "Education and Baseball" in *America* 164:13 (6 April 1991), 372-73.

[78] *Twelve Steps and Twelve Traditions*, 93-94. For "Glad Gethsemene" see Chapter 3 of this book, {XR}18.

[79] Dowling's talk to clergy in Brooklyn, 1953, "Christian Asceticism and the Twelve Steps."

[80] December 9, 1959.

[81] July 25, 1960. Now the common fact that many go through depression after facing their alcoholism is accepted. In "Darkness Visible," an article in *Vanity Fair* for December 1, 1989, William Styron speaks about his own depression hell after facing his alcoholism. Colette Dowling in *You Mean I Don't Have to Feel This Way* (New York: MacMillan, 1992) says, "The largest study ever done on psychiatric disorders in the community — not just institutions — found that half of all female alcoholics are clinically depressed. Two-thirds of those women were clinically depressed **before** they began using substances." Terry Gorski and Merlene Miller in *Staying Sober* (Independence: Herald House, 1986) include facing depression as a normal part of the recovery process, 149-155.

[82] *As Bill Sees It* (New York: AA World Services, 1967), 231.

[83] This prayer of St. Francis was framed on the fireplace wall behind Bill's desk in his study, Wit's End. Bill gave Father Ed a framed copy of the same prayer for Christmas of 1952. See Appendix B. Bill's "New Frontier" article became the centerpiece to Jack O's *Dealing with Depression in 12 Step Recovery* (Seattle: Glen Abbey Books, 1990).

[84] Ernest Kurtz, *Not God* (Center City: Hazelden, 1979).

[85] Roseann Lloyd and Merle Fossum, *True Selves: Twelve-Step Recovery from Codependency* (Center City: Hazelden, 1991). Lloyd and Fossum with stories exemplify this journey to the true self as the core of the recovery process.

[86] Bill's letter to Ollie in California, January 4, 1956.

[87] Jones to Bill W. September 1, 1953. Anne Wilson Schaef in *Beyond Therapy, Beyond Science* (San Francisco: Harper, 1992), talks of multiple addictions (268ff.) and the necessity of the teacher to be a participant. "I believe our best teachers in recovery are recovering addicts themselves and hopefully those who have moved beyond their specific addictions and are dealing with their underlying addictive process." 281. Karen Horney, in *Neurosis and Human Growth* (New York: W.W. Norton & Company, 1950) uses language in the chapters on "The Search for Glory" and "Morbid Dependency" that Bill

repeats in his letters and article on *dependency,* "The New Frontier: Emotional Sobriety."

[88] April 3, 1947.

[89] April 6, 1953.

[90] Bill's letter in New York AA Archives of May 20, 1946. Informal family groups gathered from 1941 on. It was not until 1951 that Lois and Anne B. opened a Service Office at "Stepping Stones" for 49 family groups who chose the name Al-Anon Family Groups. *Lois Remembers* (New York: Al-Anon Family Group Headquarters, Inc., 1979), 199. A history of Al-Anon Groups is in *First Steps, Al-Anon...35 Years of Beginnings* (New York: Al-Anon Family Groups, 1986).

[91] *Pass It On,* 335

[92] *Ibid.*

[93] My guess at what was indecipherable is in brackets. Dowling left words out when writing or speaking, according to Mary Louise Adams, Dowling's archivist.

[94] I am not sure what Dowling's telegraphic ending means. Is Bill "Semi" because he believes Protestant but does not worship Protestant?

[95] Xavier Leon-Dufour, *Dictionary of Biblical Theology* (New York: Seabury Press, 1967), 158.

[96] In the *Spiritual Exercises* this personal call is the meditation on the Kingdom.

[97] In 1952, Dowling sent Bill a copy of *The Spiritual Exercises of St. Ignatius* and made the same point: the need for humility in the face of power and money. He points to the Two Standards meditation again. Bill will later refer to the exact page (100) of this "Meditation on the Two Standards" in a letter to Dowling.

[98] Bill Wilson's September 1957 essay, "Let's Be Friends with Our Friends, the Clergymen."

[99] Bill asked Dowling for the *Exercises* in the letter of May 20, 1952.

[100] January 2, 1952.

[101] W. H. Longridge, *The Spiritual Exercises of Saint Ignatius of Loyola* (London: Robert Scott Roxburghe House, 1919). An updated translation of the Exercises is by David Fleming, S.J., *Contemporary Reading of the Spiritual Exercises* (St. Louis: Institute of Jesuit Sources, 1976).

[102] Tradition One: *"Our common welfare should come first; personal recovery depends upon AA unity."*

[103] *Twelve Steps and Twelve Traditions* (New York: AA World Services, 1953), 131.

[104] Jeff Smith tells John Markoe's colorful story in *From Corps to Core* (Florissant: St. Stanislaus Historical Museum, 1977). Before entering the Jesuits, John had graduated from West Point. He and his brother, William, also a Jesuit, were in trouble most of their long careers as Jesuit priests. Their problem: they campaigned for racial justice before it was politically correct.

[105] *Twelve Steps and Twelve Traditions* (New York, AA World Services, 1953), 26.

[106] *Pass It On,* Chapter 16, has a wonderful description of the time Bill heard voices who gave him their names in Nantucket. Their exact names checked out both in the graveyard and in the whaling museum.

[107] See Dowling's "A.A. Steps for the Underprivileged Non-A.A." (*Grapevine,* July 1960).

[108] #333, *Spiritual Exercises of St. Ignatius,* Fleming version.

[109] Wilkie Au, A.J., in Chapter 7, "Blessed are the Poor; Enrichment in the Midst of Privation" of *By Way of the Heart* (New York: Paulist Press, 1989), offers a modern interpretation of the Ignatian meditation on the Two Standards. Also, see page {XR}80 of this book.

[110] *Pass It On,* 312.

[111] Nell Wing in *Grateful to Have Been There* (21), remarks that Bill also learned from Lewis Browne, *This Believing World,* that too much organization, politics, money, or power would be pitfalls for groups. Milton Maxwell in his essay, "The Washingtonian Movement," from the *Quarterly Journal of Alcohol Studies,* Vol. XI, September 1950, 410-451, makes the point that the Washingtonian movement did not last because it was based on power and prestige, not anonymity.

[112] April 20, 1953.

[113] *Alcoholics Anonymous Comes of Age,* 254ff. Dowling lists the steps of God to man, beginning with the Incarnation and ending with a God who can suffer as man and be held in his mother's arms after being taken down from the cross (the Pieta).

[114] See Chapter One, "First Meeting."

[115] Appendix C, Prayer of St. Francis. The gift was two hinged frames (one containing the Prayer of St. Francis, the other a picture of St. Francis with a bird in his hand), all the size of a man's leather wallet standing long side and hinged in the middle.

[116] W. H. Longridge, *The Spiritual Exercises of St. Ignatius of Loyola* (London: Robert Roxburghe House, 1919) 159ff. Bill in his Step Eleven essay relies heavily on the imagination as a help in prayer, as does Ignatius who often begins prayer, "I will see with the eyes of the imagination."

[117] Howe goes on to say this new order is "the reconciling fellowship." *Man's Need and God's Action* (Greenwich: Seabury Press, 1953), 57.

[118] April 15, 1953.

[119] Bill will respond (February 19, 1953), "We have given the manuscript a heavy dose of chlorophyll to deaden that elder statesman smell." Dr. Tiebout, Father Ford, and Jack Alexander also checked the text.

[120] February 19, 1953.

[121] Mary Darrah in *Sister Ignatia* (Chicago: Loyola University Press, 1992) describes the attitudes of the Catholic Clergy in Chapter 6, "An Unfinished Mission: Alcoholism and Catholic Problems." Darrah tells a wonderful story of Sister Ignatia prolonging a priest's treatment stay. The rest of his group were going home. Sister Ignatia told him, "Not you though. I've dealt with your kind before. I learned a long time ago that the hardest nuts to crack in this business were clergy and doctors. Whenever I get my hands on one, he stays here twice as long." (213).

[122] *The Blue Book,* Vol. V, The Proceedings of the Fifth National Clergy Conference on Alcoholism, 152-176. Also, see the Queen's Work Pamphlet of 1947, an interview by Frank Riley of Father Ed called "Alcoholics Anonymous."

[123] *The Blue Book,* Vol. V, 164.

[124] *Ibid.*, 163. Father Ed will go on from this experience to be the first to suggest that the Twelve Steps can be used for other addictions. Father Ed Dowling, "A.A. Steps for the Underprivileged Non-A.A." (*Grapevine*, July 1960). Reprinted in *AA Today* (New York: *Grapevine*, 1960), 64.

[125] Mary Darrah in her book on Sister Ignatia tells the story of the time Sister Ignatia prayed the Stations of the Cross with Bill Wilson. "Bill began to sense a relationship between the cross of Christ and the suffering of the alcoholic." Bill identified most with Jesus being nailed to the cross (Station 11) and the plea of the dying Christ, "I thirst! My God, my God, why have you forsaken me?" 133.

[126] *The Blue Book*, Vol. V, 164.

[127] *Ibid.*

[128] *Ibid.*, 167.

[129] *Ibid.*, 171.

[130] Murray Stein, *In Mid Life* (Dallas: Spring Publications, 1983). Stein depicts Hermes as a guide for souls in mid-life crisis. Hermes is a trickster who can move between different worlds with ease. Sam Lambert, Father Ed's reporter friend, said Dowling's job at The Queen's Work was really just a cover for his real job, being an ambassador of God. Dowling's style as ambassador is close to Hermes as he moves at ease between worlds at odds with each other.

[131] April 20, 1953. Those who knew Dowling well say the beads of sweat were a sign he was in real pain from his arthritis. All this Dowling with his humor denied.

[132] May 18, 1953.

[133] See Chapter 2, {XR}10-11.

[134] Bill Wilson, "The Next Frontier: Emotional Sobriety," in *The Language of the Heart* (New York: The A.A. Grapevine Inc., 1988), 236-242.

[135] *Twelve Steps and Twelve Traditions*, 118.

[136] Ernest Kurtz, *Not God: A History of Alcoholics Anonymous* (Center City: Hazelden, 1979), 214.

[137] Wilson to Marion L., March 31, 1953.

[138] Wilson to Jeff K., April 1959. Both these letters are found on page 214 of Kurtz's *Not God.*

[139] Dowling's letter to Bill, May 25, 1953. The *Grapevine* of July 1955 has Dowling's talk on the "Three Dimensions of AA" and a reference to the same pub.

[140] From Bill's letter to Father Ed asking permission to quote this June 16, 1953. Dowling replies on July 6, 1953, with his permission to use this section in the introduction to the second edition of the Big Book.

[141] Suzanne Zuercher, O.S.B., *Enneagram Spirituality* (Notre Dame: Ave Maria Press, 1992), 119ff.

[142] Suzanne Farnham et al., *Listening Hearts: Discerning Call in Community* (Harrisburg: More House Publishing, 1991), 23.

[143] This *plan* can be seen two ways. One way is **a preconceived plan** of God eternally decreed. Another view is **mutual dialogue** as Tom Hart says in *The Art of Christian Listening* (New York: Paulist, 1980), 85. God "has not preconceived the pattern of our lives in much detail. He loves us and wants life for us; and, like good parents, he is content to give us our heads and let our choices naturally unfold out of our developing selfhood. Discernment, then, is not a magical formula for ferreting out the hidden plan, but a procedure for using our best human resources, in the context of prayerfulness and a life-orientation toward God, to frame and make those choices which seem most consonant with our selfhood and God's overarching purpose revealed in Christ."

[144] *Twelve Steps and Twelve Traditions*, 88-93.

[145] George Aschenbrenner, S.J., "Consciousness Examen" (*Review for Religious,* Vol. 31, no. 1, January 1972).

[146] John Ford, S.J., in an October 9, 1952, letter to Bill W. includes an examen for married people as something to complete the ordinary examen of consciousness. Ford says, "By the way, Helen said you were having difficulty with Step Ten. Perhaps this is where the more detailed self-examination of daily faults would come in — like St. Ignatius' daily examen of the book of Exercises."

[147] "Peace — the central sign that a call is of God. If the peace endures through ups and downs, then we have confirmation that it is authentic." *Listening Hearts,* 46.

[148] *Twelve Steps and Twelve Traditions* (New York: AA World Services Inc., 1953), 137-138 (italics mine). Bill tells this same story in *Alcoholics Anonymous Comes of Age* (New York: AA World Services, 1957), 99-102. John English, S.J., in *Spiritual Intimacy and Community* (New York: Paulist Press, 1992) treats Ignatian principles on this same issue: group discernment.

[149] *Alcoholics Anonymous Comes of Age*, 195.

[150] Mary Darrah's personal interview with Dr. Bob's son in June of 1985 as quoted in *Sister Ignatia* (Chicago: Loyola Press, 1992), 30.

[151] Father Ed continued to underline where he saw God acting in Bill's life. In an October 1, 1947 letter he concludes, "Historically, there have been superhuman interventions—yourself, Horace Crystal, the Incarnation." Joseph Tetlow confirms *desires* as the inner locus of God's action when he says, "All of our instincts, all of our desires, finally begin in God's. Somehow, back down the line, somewhere, all our desiring rises out of God's passionate desiring." *Choosing Christ in the World* (St. Louis: Institute of Jesuit Sources, 1989), 231. Also excellent on desires is Edward Kinerk, S.J.'s "Eliciting Great Desires: Their Place in the Spirituality of the Society of Jesus" (Studies in the Spirituality of Jesuits, November 1984). Harry Emerson Fosdick in *The Meaning of Prayer* (Association Press, 1915), claims the importance of "dominant desire" as the place where prayer begins. Desires and choices are key to recovery.

[152] The fullest explanation of both are in two books by Jules Toner, S.J.: *A Commentary of St. Ignatius' Rules for the Discernment of Spirits* (St. Louis: Institute of Jesuit Sources, 1982) and *Discerning God's Will* (St. Louis: Institute of Jesuit Sources, 1991). A short popular version of this material is in Chris Aridas's *Discernment: Seeking God in Every Situation* (New York: Living Flame Press, 1980).

[153] March 14, 1942, letter to Peter Brooks, S.J., Missouri Province Provincial of Jesuits and a classmate of Father Ed's.

[154] May 27, 1942, letter to Bill W. from Father Ed as quoted at the end of Chapter 4 in this book.

[155] January 2, 1952.

[156] Dean Brackley, S.J., has an updated presentation of this meditation with social and historical dimensions in *Studies in the Spirituality of Jesuits*, January 1988. Bill W. offers his own image of the Devil's call in Appendix F, his allegory of fool's gold in his essay, "Humility for Today."

[157] *St. Ignatius' Own Story* translated by William J. Young, S.J. (Chicago: Loyola University Press, 1956), 10.

[158] *Ibid.,* 2.

[159] See Chapter 9 of this book, "The Spiritual Exercises and The Traditions," {XR} pp 73ff.

[160] Letter from Father Ed to Bill W., July 24, 1952.

[161] Chapter 13 of this book, "A Softer, Easier Way: The LSD Experiment."

[162] These thirty letters cover from February 21, 1955, to May of 1958.

[163] Christmas 1955.

[164] July 13, 1955.

[165] July 26, 1955.

[166] July 19, 1955. Lois with Al-Anon pioneered a breakthrough for family recovery. This story is told in *First Steps Al-Anon: 35 Years of Beginnings* (New York: Al-Anon Family HQO, 1986).

[167] Appendix B, "Why Alcoholics Anonymous is Anonymous" by Bill in *Alcoholics Anonymous Comes of Age* (New York: Alcoholics Anonymous World Services, Inc., 1957), 286-294. See Bill's "Humility for Today" in *The Language of the Heart,* 254ff.

[168] *Ibid.,* 286

[169] *Ibid.,* 294.

[170] *Twelve Steps and Twelve Traditions* (New York: Alcoholics Anonymous World Services, Inc., 1953), 187.

[171] July 19, 1955.

[172] July 13, 1955.

[173] July 14, 1955. Dowling had memorized Thompson's "The Hound of Heaven."

[174] Chapter 8, {XR}51.

175 *Alcoholics Anonymous Comes of Age,* 258-59.

176 *Ibid,* 257-261

177 *Ibid,* 256.

178 October 11, 1960.

179 Queen's Work Newsletter in an article by Dowling called "How to Win Friends."

180 Act I, Scene 3. Burnham, the maiden name of Lois, came from an English family, in the area of England referred to in *Macbeth* as Burnham Wood according to Paul Lang, archivist at Stepping Stones.

181 June 2, 1958.

182 See Father Ed's *Grapevine* article (July 1960), "A.A. Steps for the Underprivileged Non-A.A."

183 September 2, 1958.

184 June 2, 1959 letter. Thomas E. Powers, *Invitation to a Great Experiment* (New York: Doubleday & Company, Inc., 1979). This is a reissue of *First Questions on the Life of the Spirit* (New York: Harper & Row, 1959). A chapter on the "Practice of Ego Reduction" challenges the reader to take a chance on God and offers suggestions to keep "on the Way"; how to avoid falling off or drifting away.

185 June 16, 1959.

186 June 22, 1959.

187 June 29, 1959.

188 October 12, 1959.

189 October 8, 1957, Bill W. letter to Joe Dingles, Dowling's former student.

190 Nell Wing, *Grateful to Have Been There* (Chicago: Parkside Publishing Corporation, 1992), 54-55. Cf. Chapter 23 of *Pass It On.* These experiments were before all mood-altering chemicals had been linked as addictive and had a "bad name."

191 Letter of November 23, 1959, from Bill W. to Dowling.

¹⁹² This letter is not available. Sam Shoemaker had consulted Episcopal Bishop Pardue. The Bishop declared himself "in the utmost sympathy with what [Bill] is doing." The Bishop was convinced that half our problems are biochemical and do not go back to sin and cannot wholly be governed by prayer. E. Kurtz offered me this information from Charles Knippel's dissertation (St. Louis University, 1987), "Samuel M. Shoemaker's Theological Influence on William G. Wilson's Twelve Step Spiritual Program of Recovery."

¹⁹³ November 23, 1959.

¹⁹⁴ *Pass It On,* 371.

¹⁹⁵ November 23, 1959.

¹⁹⁶ November 23, 1959.

¹⁹⁷ This letter is not available.

¹⁹⁸ Again Dowling refers to the seeming good promise of the witches, which led Macbeth to murder the king, Duncan. Again, Dowling pointed to honors leading to pride and all other evils, the lesson of the Ignatian meditation on the Two Standards. Dowling, as Ignatius, recognized the reality of an evil principle.

¹⁹⁹ December 14, 1959. Dowling quoted from the Longridge edition of the Spiritual Exercises which he gave Bill, 192-193. Two excellent modern commentaries on this discernment rule can be found in *The Way of Ignatius Loyola,* ed. Philip Sheldrake, S.J. (St. Louis: The Institute of Jesuit Sources, 1991) in Chapter 14, "The Serpent's Tail: Rules for Discernment," by David Lonsdale and "Structure of the Rules for Discernment" by Michael Buckley.

²⁰⁰ Father Ed had quoted this poem, "The Hound of Heaven" by Francis Thompson, at the 1955 AA Convention. This quote, his favorite, he used often on Christmas letters.

²⁰¹ This 1958 conference came up with a compromise solution; it was not until 1967 that the Conference voted for a majority of alcoholic trustees.

²⁰² June 2, 1958. This is Bill's letter to Father Ed about the conflicts in the AA Conference.

²⁰³ December 29, 1958. Bill writes about these beginnings in *The AA Service Manual and Twelve Concepts for World Service.*

²⁰⁴ March 17, 1960.

[205] See Appendix F, Father Ed's Biographical Sheet.

[206] He had talked late into the night with Cana and AA friends at the home of a family where he stayed.

[207] "To Father Ed — Godspeed!" by Bill W.

[208] April 4, 1960

[209] May 27, 1942, letter from Father Ed to Bill W.

[210] Father Fred Zimmerman, S.J., in a July 16, 1986, letter to Father Jim Egan, S.J.

Appendix A

A.A. Steps for the Underprivileged Non-A.A.

By Edward J. Dowling, S.J.

(A longtime friend of AA shows how the Twelve Steps can be effectively applied to any problem in life.)

More influential on history than the Nile or the Mississippi, is another river — the Gulf Stream. Without it the British Isles would be as bleak as Labrador or Siberia.

AA is like a Gulf Stream in the ocean of today's life. It is indistinguishable from its banks — but its winds, like burnt incense, whisper hope and life to human Siberias.

"It's like AA" has been the passport to acceptance among the dignosclerotic (hardening of the dignity) for such stigma-pilloried movements as Narcotics Anonymous, Crime Prevention, Recovery, Inc., Divorcees Anonymous, Divorcees Unanimous, WANA, Adiposics Anonymous, the Mattachine Society, Average People, Nicotinic Nobodies, Daughters of Bilitis, Gamblers Anonymous, Check Writers Anonymous, Security Cloister, Politicians Anonymous, and other self-help groups in areas of varying degrees of seriousness and helplessness.

Definitions of Twelfth Step words in the Twelve Steps suggest the extent of the application of these Steps to non-alcoholics.

Sanity in the Second Step agrees with psychiatrists' classification of alcoholism as a psychosis. If these steps can arrest one psychosis, why not other psychoses and neuroses? At least two groups, "Security Cloister" and "Average People" use AA's Twelve Steps as a filter for spiritual and religious helps in arresting neuroses and psychoses.

Alcohol is a narcotic. Narcotics Anonymous members use the Twelve Steps.

Alcoholism is, when unchecked, *gluttony* for alcoholic drink. AA's success with this type of gluttony opens new hope for the better known gluttony, which is killing many people — respectfully autopsied as obesity or overweight.

My 240-pound gluttony gave me two heart attacks. An alcoholic doctor got me down toward 180 when he advised a total AA abstinence from starch, butter, salt and sugar. He said these four foods were probably my "alcohol." Abstinence was so much easier than temperance. The "balanced" diet often prescribed was loaded with these four "craving-creating appetizers." I was like a lush tapering off on martinis. Only after the discovery of the AA approach to craving-creating intake did I realize that the Jesuit Ignatius' first rule for diet in his Spiritual Exercises was to go easy on craving-creating food and drink.

AA's success with liquid gluttony opens up a hope, not only for solid gluttony, but also for the larger class of body compulsions of which gluttony is a species. Gluttony is a species of sensuality or inordinate body drives. Unarrested alcoholism is sensuality. Sensuality covers such situations as too many cancer-threatening cigarettes and qualitative or quantitative sex deviations. I have seen, in one case, the arresting of sexual deviation and resultant normal behavior through the help of the AA Steps in a non-alcoholic man. I have seen a compulsive infatuation (with its sensual concomitants and addiction) yield to the AA Steps. Some ten years ago I arrested my own nicotinic addiction with the help of the AA Steps.

In moving their therapy from the expensive clinical couch to the low-cost coffee bar, from the inexperienced professional to the amateur expert, AA has democratized sanity.

As Columbus, Marquette, and Lewis and Clark pushed toward the terminals of our frontier, so AA has advanced the frontiers of hope even in situations otherwise "powerless."

The psychiatrist has alerted the non-psychiatric doctor to the psychic dimension of somatic disorders. AA alerted both to a third dimension, the spiritual or religious, and pioneered an ethnic-psycho-somatic therapy. That means that the cure for the shakes is via the shaker's belief in God.

Psychiatrists alerted the clergy to the "cause and cure significance" of the spiritual or psychic. AA helped them even more by demonstrating the "cause and cure significance" of religion. The agnostic smog of urban materialism had corroded religious heirlooms of many spiritually impoverished people. Yet it was in the sophisticated urban saloons that those religious values were recovered by many. Roger Babson's dictum, "the greatest of our undeveloped resources is faith," suggests the profound contribution that the AA Second Step has made to many. The dramatic ethical focus in many lives that resulted has salvaged many ergs of wasted effort.

Sometimes non-AA members of an AA family are quicker to understand the Twelfth Step application of these principles to all our affairs than is the AA, who is transfixed in the absorbing contemplation of his new sanity, social life and psychiatric-sacerdotal role. Possibly, if the AA spent less time and energy in the breadth dimension of spreading AA and more in the length and depth dimension, the breadth of its spread might not be limited to such a low percentage of the world's alcoholics. The length dimension means the application of these Steps to *all our affairs*— sedatives, tensions, compulsions, and so on. The depth dimension is suggested by the Eleventh Step, "sought through meditation...for knowledge of His will for us and the power to carry that out."

Father Ed, an early and wonderful friend of AA, died as this last message to us went to press. He was the greatest and most gentle soul that I may ever know. Bill W.

Reprinted with permission from *The Grapevine,* July 1960.

Appendix B

How to Enjoy Being Miserable

by Edward Dowling, S.J.

There are two kinds of misery.

Self-chosen. Doing without candy or smoking. Probably very unimportant, compared to the second kind.

God-chosen, or providential. Friday abstinence, headaches, sister-in-law's temper, weather, death. These can be either:

Big. Too rare and overwhelming to enjoy until we have gradually learned by practice on little sufferings how to do it.

Little. Very important, because petty inconveniences and annoyances are a thousand times more frequent than big tragedies. Like the widow and her mite, usually we have only a mite of suffering, like a traffic delay or a telephone busy signal to offer. Little sufferings are easier to practice on in order to develop an habitual outlook and attitude toward inevitable misery. There are three attitudes possible. We can

Be Crushed by them and jump into the river or a movie or into a debauch of self-pity, profanity or resentment.

Accept them resignedly. If we ignore them stoically we are wasting a most valuable experience. It would be like ignoring your pay check. If we try to be spartanly gallant, soon our nerves will get frayed and we will end up by being crushed by our woes.

Enjoy them. To do this you have to be either crazy or in love. In everyday life we see instances of people wanting pain if it helps someone they love. In carrying a trunk upstairs with your mother, you definitely want to get the heavy end of the burden. On a winter night a mother will shiver so as to give a warm blanket to her child. Hence the psychological trick of changing from resigned willing acceptance of suffering, to grateful wanting to take up and enjoy suffering consists in finding someone we love who will be helped by our sufferings. St. Paul supplies that person when he points out the chance we have to "fill up those things that are wanting of the sufferings of Christ." This grateful wanting and enjoyment of suffering is

NOT in our FEELINGS. Christ in Gethsemane or a patient in a dentist's chair are examples of a person's will wanting to do things which his feelings do not want.

BUT in our WILL which is the essential determinant of virtue and vice, of misery and joy. A little insurance against feeling that you are insincere in your will's act of gratitude for suffering can be had by momentarily placing your hand to your breast to accompany your aspiration of gratitude, since this is an external action which cannot be done without an act of the will. Even in this matter of the will's gratitude for and want of suffering, it is psychologically important to realize that our little act of gratitude for a snub or a splinter means

NOT that I want the suffering to continue, because as far as I know I may be dead the next instant and it may be God's will that the suffering cease. Nor does it mean that I want the suffering to be worse than it is, because the amount I have is the exact amount that God wills.

BUT in the specific instant, now, since I cannot avoid this suffering, I want to get the best possible use out of it. The Devil will try to frighten you by directing your attention to the future and pointing out how terrible it will be if this suffering continues. Tell him to go to hell. Screwtape, the old business agent of the Devil's Union, says that since the present is the only point at which time touches eternity, humans should be tempted to live in the past or, better still, in the future, where most vices, such as fear, avarice, lust, and ambition draw their strength. According to Screwtape Letters, the Devil's delight is a human soul "hag-ridden by the future — haunted by visions of imminent heaven or hell on earth."

To Sum Up. There are five psychological steps in this technique of learning how to enjoy being miserable. Not self-chosen, but God-chosen sufferings. Not big, but little suffering. Not gallant willingness, but grateful wanting. Not feelings, but will. Not future, but present.

Thoreau's remark that "all men lead lives of quiet desperation," can be paralleled by the chronic alert loneliness of all women. To these chronic discouragements and lonelinesses we can add, this Christmas time, the acute anxiety and futility that brood over a confused war-tense world.

Strangely, these three sufferings — loneliness ("Couldn't you watch an hour with Me?"), discouragement (Isaiah said Christ took upon Himself the sickening responsibility for "the iniquity of us all"), the futility (What's-the-use?) engulfed God in Gethsemane in that rendezvous where Divinity came closest to me. Where God's loneliness and mine are bridged by St. Paul's union of suffering, I can find the closest approach to God, to power, to achievement, to happiness, to joy!

The enjoyment of misery is not the fanaticism of the pervert nor the occasional luxury of the ecstatic. Rather, it is the everyday necessity of the weakest and the worst of us or we will grow weaker and worse, and perish. Even if we could outdo Christ in generosity, what better use could we make of the hundred little daily inconveniences than to use them to buy stock in Christ's venture of Gethsemane and Calvary?

This 1954 world *is* the passion. Any hour in any place is Gethsemane. The joys of the first Christmas were accompanied by, if not rooted in, misery — the damp, cold night, the inhospitality that poor relatives always get, the discomfort and dirt of the donkey, the roads and the cave, the loneliness and awe that young mothers have always felt at the coming of their firstborn — who will say that these are not the things that have brought to a sore, sick world the merriment and the joys of Christmas?

This Christmas will bring to those who look for the secret of Christmas merriment and joy the plea of Christ "to watch an hour with Me." And the closer the friendship, the more of His suffering and misery He will ask you to share.

May you enjoy a miserable Christmas! No other kind can really be merry.

Action Now, Vol. 8, Dec. 1954, No. 3.

Appendix C

Prayer of St. Francis

Lord, make me an instrument of Your peace.
Where there is hatred, let me sow love;
Where there is injury, pardon;
Where there is doubt, faith;
Where there is despair, hope;
Where there is darkness, light;
And where there is sadness, joy.
O, Divine Master, grant that I
may not so much seek
To be consoled as to console;
To be understood as to understand;
To be loved as to love;
For it is in giving that we receive.
It is in pardoning that we are pardoned;
And it is in dying that we are born to eternal life.
Saint Francis

Appendix D

*The Next Frontier —
Emotional Sobriety*

I think that many oldsters who have put our A.A. "booze cure" to severe but successful tests still find they often lack emotional sobriety. Perhaps they will be the spearhead for the next major development in A.A. — the development of much more real maturity and balance (which is to say, humility) in our relations with ourselves, with our fellows, and with God.

Those adolescent urges that so many of us have for top approval, perfect security and perfect romance — urges quite appropriate to age seventeen — prove to be an impossible way of life when we are at age forty-seven or fifty-seven.

Since A.A. began, I've taken immense wallops in all these areas because of my failure to grow up emotionally and spiritually. My God, how painful it is to keep demanding the impossible, and how very painful to discover finally that all along we have had the cart before the horse! Then comes the final agony of seeing how awfully wrong we have been, but still finding ourselves unable to get off the emotional merry-go-round.

How to translate a right mental conviction into a right emotional result, and so into easy, happy and good living — well, that's not only the neurotic's problem, it's the problem of life itself for all of us who have got to the point of real willingness to hew to right principles in all our affairs.

Even then as we hew away, peace and joy will still elude us. That's the place so many of A.A. oldsters have come to. And it's a hell of a spot, literally. How shall our unconscious — from which so many of our fears, compulsions and phony aspirations still stream — be brought into line with what we actually believe, know and want! How to convince our dumb, raging and hidden "Mr. Hyde" becomes our main task.

I've recently come to believe that this can be achieved. I believe so because I begin to see many benighted ones — folks like you and me — commencing to get results. Last autumn [several years back — *ed.*] depression having no really rational cause at all, almost took me to the cleaners. I began to be scared that I was in for another long chronic spell. Considering the grief I've had with depressions, it wasn't a bright prospect.

I kept asking myself, "Why can't the Twelve Steps work to release depression?" By the hour I stared at the St. Francis Prayer... "It's better to comfort than to be comforted." Here was the formula, all right. But why didn't it work?

Suddenly I realized what the matter was. My basic flaw had always been dependence — almost absolute dependence — on people or circumstances to supply me with prestige, security and the like. Failing to get these things according to my perfectionist dreams and specifications, I had fought for them. And when defeat came, so did my depression.

There wasn't a chance of making the outgoing love of St. Francis a workable and joyous way of life until these fatal and almost absolute dependencies were cut away.

Because I had over the years undergone a little spiritual development, the *absolute* quality of these frightful dependencies had never before been so starkly revealed. Reinforced by what Grace I could secure in prayer, I found I had to exert every ounce of will and action to cut off these faulty emotional dependencies upon people, upon A.A., indeed upon any set of circumstances whatsoever.

Then only could I be free to love as Francis had. Emotional and instinctual satisfactions, I saw, were really the extra dividends of having love, offering love, and expressing a love appropriate to each relationship of life.

Plainly I could not avail myself of God's love until I was able to offer it back to Him by loving others as He would have me. And I couldn't possibly do that so long as I was victimized by false dependencies.

For my dependency meant demand — a demand for the possession and control of the people and the conditions surrounding me.

While those words "absolute dependency" may look like a gimmick, they were the ones that helped to trigger my release into my present degree of stability and quietness of mind, qualities which I am now trying to consolidate by offering love to others regardless of the return to me.

This seems to be the primary healing circuit — an outgoing love of God's creation and His people, by means of which we avail ourselves of His love for us. It is most clear that the real current can't flow until our paralyzing dependencies are broken, and broken at depth. Only then can we possibly have a glimmer of what adult love really is.

Spiritual calculus, you say? Not a bit of it. Watch any A.A. of six months working with a new Twelfth Step case. If the case says "To the devil with you," the Twelfth Stepper only smiles and turns to another case. He doesn't feel frustrated or rejected. If his next case responds and in turn starts to give love and attention to other alcoholics, yet gives none back to him, the sponsor is happy about it anyway. He still doesn't feel rejected; instead he rejoices that his one-time prospect is sober and happy. And if his next following case turns out in later time to be his best friend (or romance), then the sponsor is most joyful. But he well knows that his happiness is a by-product — the extra dividend of giving without any demand for a return.

The really stabilizing thing for him was having and offering love to that strange drunk on his doorstep. That was Francis at work, powerful and practical, minus dependency and minus demand.

In the first six months of my own sobriety, I worked hard with many alcoholics. Not a one responded. Yet this work kept me sober. It wasn't a question of those alcoholics giving me anything. My stability came out of trying to give, not out of demanding that I receive.

Thus I think it can work out with emotional sobriety. If we examine every disturbance we have, great or small, we will find at the root of it some unhealthy dependency and its consequent unhealthy demand. Let us, with God's help, continually surrender these hobbling demands. Then we can be set free to live and love; we may then be able to Twelfth Step ourselves and others into emotional sobriety.

Of course I haven't offered you a really new idea—only a gimmick that has started to unhook several of my own "hexes" at depth. Nowadays my brain no longer races compulsively in either elation, grandiosity or depression. I have been given a quiet place in bright sunshine.

Reprinted with permission from *The Grapevine,* January 1958.

Appendix E

The Twelve Steps of Alcoholics Anonymous

1.   We admitted we were powerless over alcohol — that our lives had become unmanageable.
2.   Came to believe that a Power greater than ourselves could restore us to sanity.
3.   Made a decision to turn our will and our lives over to the care of God *as we understood Him.*
4.   Made a searching and fearless moral inventory of ourselves.
5.   Admitted to God, to ourselves, and to another human being the exact nature of our wrongs.
6.   Were entirely ready to have God remove all these defects of character.
7.   Humbly asked Him to remove our shortcomings.
8.   Made a list of all persons we had harmed, and became willing to make amends to them all.
9.   Made direct amends to such people wherever possible, except when to do so would injure them or others.
10.   Continued to take personal inventory and when we were wrong promptly admitted it.
11.   Sought through prayer and meditation to improve our conscious contact with God *as we understood Him,* praying only for knowledge of His will for us and the power to carry that out.
12.   Having had a spiritual awakening as the result of these steps, we tried to carry this message to alcoholics and to practice these principles in all our affairs.

The Twelve Traditions of Alcoholics Anonymous

1. Our common welfare should come first; personal recovery depends upon A.A. unity.
2. For our group purpose there is but one ultimate authority — a loving God as He may express Himself in our group conscience. Our leaders are but trusted servants; they do not govern.
3. The only requirement for A.A. membership is a desire to stop drinking.
4. Each group should be autonomous except in matters affecting other groups or A.A. as a whole.
5. Each group has but one primary purpose — to carry its message to the alcoholic who still suffers.
6. An A.A. group ought never endorse, finance or lend the A.A. name to any related facility or outside enterprise, lest problems of money, property and prestige divert us from our primary purpose.
7. Every A.A. group ought to be fully self-supporting, declining outside contributions.
8. Alcoholics Anonymous should remain forever nonprofessional, but our service centers may employ special workers.
9. A.A., as such, ought never be organized; but we may create service boards or committees directly responsible to those they serve.
10. Alcoholics Anonymous has no opinion on outside issues; hence the A.A. name ought never be drawn into public controversy.
11. Our public relations policy is based on attraction rather than promotion; we need always maintain personal anonymity at the level of press, radio and films.
12. Anonymity is the spiritual foundation of all our Traditions, ever reminding us to place principles before personalities.

*The Twelve Steps of A.A. are taken from *Alcoholics Anonymous,* 3d ed., published by A.A. World Serivces, Inc., New York, N.Y., 564. Reprinted with permission of A.A. World Services, Inc. (See editor's note on copyright page.)

Appendix F

REV. EDWARD DOWLING, S.J.
  Associate Editor of the Queen's Work
  Director, Cana Department, Sodalities of Our Lady
  Office and Residence—3115 South Grand Blvd., St. Louis, Mo.
BIOGRAPHY

1898, Sept. 1	Born, St. Louis, Mo.
1913-16	Summer work as factory laborer
1918	U.S. Army—Private
1918-1919	Reporter, *St. Louis Globe Democrat*
1919	Entered Jesuit Order at Florissant, Mo.
1926-29	Teacher at Loyola Academy, Chicago, Ill.
1931	Ordained at St. Louis by Archbishop Glennon
1932-1960	Staff of Central Office of Sodality of Our Lady
1934-1960	Faculty, Summer School of Catholic Action
[1960, April 3	Died at Memphis, Tenn.]
[1960, April 6	Buried at St. Stanislaus Cemetery, Florissant.]

EDUCATION
  Baden Public and Holy Name Parochial Schools, St. Louis
  St. Louis University High School
  St. Louis University, A.B., 1924; M.A., 1925
  St. Stanislaus Seminary, Cleveland, Ohio
  St. Mary's College, St. Mary's, Kans.
  Medill School of Journalism, Northwestern University, Evanston, Ill.
OFFICIAL
  First President, St. Louis Housing Authority (past)
  Honorary Vice President, National Municipal League (past)
  Council, Proportional Representation League
  Advisory Council, Quill and Scroll (past)

Faculty, traveling Summer School of Catholic Action (about 25 cities in U.S. and Canada)

Faculty, Maryville College, St. Louis, Mo. (past)

Steering Committee, Missouri Council of Family Relations

Sponsor of Alcoholics Anonymous, Recovery, Inc., Proportional Representation Elections, Cana Conference Movement (has given about 300 Cana Conferences in 30 states and Canada)

Delegate to Toronto and San Francisco conventions, American Newspaper Guild

Delegate to Oxford, England, and Rome, Italy, conventions of International Union of Family Organizations, representing National Council of Family Relations and Family Life Bureau, National Catholic Welfare Conference

Member Advisory Board, Family Life Bureau

MEMBERSHIPS

Proportional Representation Society of Great Britain

Old Catlow Society of Ireland

American Political Science Association

American Irish Historical Society

National Council of Family Relations

National Press Club

Sigma Delta Chi

Missouri Council of Family Relations

Missouri State Historical Society

Missouri Athletic Club

Public Questions Club of St. Louis

Old Baden Society

St. Louis Railway Enthusiasts Club

TRAVEL

Canada, Mexico, Ireland, England, Germany, Italy, Portugal, Spain, France

(Cf. *Catholic Who's Who, Who's Who Clergy, International Who's Who, Directory of American Political Science Assn.*)

Appendix G

Humility for Today

When I inventory such defects, I like to draw a picture and tell myself a story. My picture is that of a Highway to Humility, and my story is an allegory. On one side of my Highway, I see a great bog. The Highway's edge borders a shallow marsh which finally shelves down into that muddy morass of guilt and rebellion in which I have so often floundered. Self-destruction lies in wait out there, and I know this. But the country on the other side of the road looks fine. I see inviting glades and beyond them great mountains. The countless trails leading into this pleasant land look safe. It will be easy, I think, to find one's way back.

Together with numbers of friends, I decide to take a brief detour. We pick our path and happily plunge along it. Elatedly, somebody soon says, "Maybe we'll find gold on top of that mountain." Then to our amazement we do strike gold — not nuggets in the streams, but fully minted coins. The heads of these coins each declare, "This is pure gold — twenty-four carats." Surely, we think this is the reward for our patient plodding back there in the everlasting brightness of the Highway.

Soon, though, we begin to notice the words on the tails of our coins and we have strange forebodings: some pieces carry other attractive inscriptions. "I am Power," "I am Acclaim," "I am Wealth," "I am Righteousness," they say. But others seem very strange. For example: "I am the Master Race," "I am the Benefactor," "I am Good Causes," "I am God." This is very puzzling. Nevertheless we pocket them. But next come real shockers. They read: "I'm Pride," "I'm Revenge," "I'm Disunity," "I'm Chaos." Then we turn up a single coin — just one — which declares: "I am the Devil himself." Some of us are horrified and we cry, "This is fool's gold, and this is a fool's paradise — let's clear out of here!"

But many would not return with us. They said, "Let's stay here and sort over those damned coins. We'll pick only the ones that carry the lucky inscriptions. For instance, those that say, 'Power and Glory' and 'Righteousness.' You fellows are going to be sorry you didn't stick around." Not strangely, it was years before this part of our original company returned to the Highway.

They told us the story of those who had sworn never to return. They had said, "This money is real gold, and don't tell us any different. We're going to pile up all we can. Sure, we don't like those fool mottoes. But there's plenty of firewood here. We'll just melt all this stuff down into good solid gold bricks." Then our late arrivals added: "This is how the gold of Pride claimed our brothers. They were already quarreling over their bricks when we left. Some were hurt and a few were dying. They had begun to destroy each other."

This symbolic picture graphically tells me that I may attain "humility for today" only to the extent that I am able to avoid the bog of guilt and rebellion, and that fair but deceiving land which is strewn with the coin of Pride. This is how I can find and stay on the Road to Humility which lies in between. Therefore, a constant inventory which can reveal when I am off the road is always in order.

Bill Wilson, "Humility for Today" (June 1961) in *The Language of the Heart*, pp. 255-259.

Other titles that will interest you...

Not-God

A History of Alcoholics Anonymous
  by Ernest Kurtz, Ph.D.
  Thorough, comprehensive, and candid, this is the story of Alcoholics Anonymous. Ernest Kurtz documents the history of A.A., placing the development of the fellowship within the larger framework of a changing America. In *Not-God*, Kurtz creates both an absorbing story and a compelling historical work. 436 pp.
Order No. 1036

Grateful to Have Been There

My 42 Years with Bill and Lois, and the Evolution of Alcoholics Anonymous
  by Nell Wing
  For 20 years, Nell Wing worked as an aide and executive secretary to Bill W., co-founder of Alcoholics Anonymous, and was a close friend of Lois W., co-founder of Al-Anon. An A.A. researcher, secretary, publications editor, and archivist, she shares forty-two years of personal memories and impressions of Lois and Bill and their work in the recovery movement. 150 pp.
Order No. 7808

About Hazelden Publishing

As part of the Hazelden Betty Ford Foundation, Hazelden Publishing offers both cutting-edge educational resources and inspirational books. Our print and digital works help guide individuals in treatment and recovery, and their loved ones. Professionals who work to prevent and treat addiction also turn to Hazelden Publishing for evidence-based curricula, digital content solutions, and videos for use in schools, treatment programs, correctional programs, and electronic health records systems. We also offer training for implementation of our curricula.

Through published and digital works, Hazelden Publishing extends the reach of healing and hope to individuals, families, and communities affected by addiction and related issues.

For more information about Hazelden publications,
please call **800-328-9000**
or visit us online at **hazelden.org/bookstore.**